Charles A. Lindbergh

Walter L. Hixson
University of Akron

Charles A. Lindbergh
Lone Eagle
Third Edition

THE LIBRARY OF AMERICAN BIOGRAPHY

Edited by Mark C. Carnes

PEARSON
Longman

New York   Boston   San Francisco
London   Toronto   Sydney   Tokyo   Singapore   Madrid
Mexico City   Munich   Paris   Cape Town   Hong Kong   Montreal

Acquisitions Editor: Michael Boezi
Executive Marketing Manager: Sue Westmoreland
Production Coordinator: Virginia Riker
Electronic Page Makeup: Alison Barth Burgoyne
Cover Design Manager: John Callahan
Cover Photo: ©Bettmann Collection / CORBIS
Photo Researcher: Photosearch, Inc.
Photo Researcher: Chrissy McIntyre
Senior Manufacturing Buyer: Alfred C. Dorsey

Library of Congress Cataloging-in-Publication Data

Hixson, Walter L.
    Charles A. Lindbergh, lone eagle / Walter L. Hixson. -- 3rd ed.
        p. cm. -- (Library of American biography)
    Includes bibliographical references and index.
    ISBN 0-321-09323-2
    1. Lindbergh, Charles A. (Charles Augustus), 1902–1974. 2. Air
pilots--United States--Biography. I. Title. II. Title: Lone eagle.
III. Series: Library of American biography (New York, N.Y.)

TL540.L5H45 2006
629.13092--dc22   2006001208

Visit us at www.ablongman.com

ISBN 0–321–09323–2

Contents

Editor's Preface

Philip Roth's novel, *The Plot Against America* (2004), was a curious best-seller. Most historical novels draw readers into the past. But Roth's novel, though festooned with the details of history, narrated a story that did not occur. Charles A. Lindbergh did not defeat Franklin D. Roosevelt in 1940, and the plot—a Nazi takeover of the United States—never happened.

What made the novel compelling was the hypothetical shiver it elicited in readers, many of whom thought that, yes, it might have happened here. Lindbergh, the aviator-hero, might have run for president in 1940 and defeated Roosevelt; and Lindbergh, a well-known anti-Semite, might have become a Nazi stooge; and Hitler and Goering might have transformed the United States into another province of the Third Reich.

Walter Hixson's biography of Lindbergh shows why this was implausible. Lindbergh did indeed become, as Hixson puts it, "a wildly acclaimed national hero" following his solo trans-Atlantic flight in 1927; and the young aviator's image loomed even larger during the Depression, when Americans desperately needed someone to look up to. But Lindbergh's opposition to American intervention in World War II elicited no outpouring of national support. Hixson shows, on the contrary, that Lindbergh was widely condemned as an alleged appeaser and Nazi sympathizer. Once a cultural embodiment of hope, Lindbergh now experienced vilification as a "virtual traitor."

The charges were unfair. Though opposed to the war, Lindbergh worked for the war effort. "I have always believed that every American citizen had the right and duty to state his opinion in peace and to fight for his country in war," he said. He even flew secret combat missions against the Japanese. After the war, too, Lindbergh proved he was no one's stooge. Initially a proponent of technology and its boundless promise, Lindbergh came to embrace environmentalism and sympathize with the plight of indigenous peoples throughout the world.

"These themes of the relationship of the individual to mass society, the desire for individual heroes, and environmentalism versus 'progress' have contemporary relevance," Hixson observes. "The right to speak out against foreign policy and especially going to war—and the criticism of those who do so—is very much still with us today," Hixson adds.

The story of Charles A. Lindbergh was indeed remarkable. As Hixson shows in this forthright and even-handed biography, it requires no fictional embellishment.

MARK C. CARNES

Author's Preface

I became interested in Charles A. Lindbergh in the course of my work as a historian of U.S. foreign relations. I wondered how the boy-hero of the 1920s had become one of the most vilified figures in the country on the eve of American intervention in World War II. While it was Lindbergh's views on foreign policy that first attracted my attention, as I began to do research I discovered that his whole life had unfolded like an epic drama. He rose from obscurity to the height of glory, before descending to the depths of tragedy and obloquy. The fame Lindbergh achieved in 1927 has obscured a proper understanding of him. While the public and the media expected him to play the role of popular hero, Lindbergh was an uncompromising individualist.

Colleagues, family, and friends helped me in coming to terms with my subject. Roger Grant and James Richardson offered insightful criticism of the first draft of the book. Oscar Handlin proved to be a superb editor. Randy Roberts and Michael S. Sherry also helped me in revising the work. Justus Doenecke went to extraordinary efforts to point out factual errors, guide me to relevant literature, and challenge interpretations. The new Series Editor, Mark C. Carnes, has refreshed the series with an eye towards the needs of the undergrad student. The new set of Study & Discussion Questions included at the end of the book serve as evidence to that fact.

Family members who helped me in various ways during the course of this project include Allie, Clarence, Emma, Kandy, and William F. Hixson; Traci and Tom Barracato; Ashley, Keith, Kendra, and Tania Ahlborn; and John Azzolini and Anne Clotfelter.

All the individuals cited above have improved the book; none is responsible for my interpretations or any errors that might remain.

Walter L. Hixson

Charles A. Lindbergh

1

The Lindberghs of Minnesota

In 1859 Ola Mansson decided he had little choice but to take his family and leave their home in Sweden. He quickly concluded that the only suitable place for them to relocate was the "glorious New Scandinavia," the American state of Minnesota. Mansson, a banker and reform politician who served twelve years in the *Rikstag,* the Swedish parliament, had fallen afoul of political enemies. Among the issues that enraged them, along with his campaign for broader suffrage and improvements in public transit, was his insistence that the whipping post was a remnant of barbarism and should be abandoned for more modern methods of criminal punishment.

Director of a loan office in Malmö, a major city in southern Sweden, Mansson had committed technical errors relating to the bank's finances. His political foes seized this opportunity, accused Mansson of embezzlement, saw to his conviction, and left him feeling he had little choice but to leave the country. His first wife having died, Mansson undertook the journey to America with his second wife, Louisa, twenty years his junior, and their infant son, Charles Augustus, named for the new Swedish king. Arriving in New York after a six-week crossing, the fifty-year-old Mansson did what was common among immigrants to

America—he changed his name. He chose August as his given name and Lindbergh as the family surname.

After a long train ride from New York City to Chicago and then to Dubuque, Iowa, the Lindberghs boarded a riverboat for a trip up the Mississippi to St. Paul. From there they moved to rural Stearns County, north of the Twin Cities of Minneapolis and St. Paul, and began to dig out a living from the hard ground of rural Minnesota. The Lindberghs had little remaining cash, which compelled Louisa to sell her gold watch for a cow so they could at least have milk to drink. The family settled among a community of Swedish immigrants. August constructed a crude, 12-by-16-foot log cabin and began farming. After two years in America, he decided to build a frame house, but nearly died in the process. While helping to saw logs at a local mill, August slipped and fell onto a jagged blade, breaking several ribs and shredding his right arm. He had to ride more than thirty miles and wait three days before a doctor could see him. His arm amputated at the shoulder, the Swede clung to life and eventually recovered.

As a result of the accident, the burdens of providing for the family fell on August's young son, Charles August. Virtually from the moment he could walk, the boy was shooting his rifle. Fish and game, especially deer, were so plentiful that he never failed to provide food for the table. He often took overnight trips to town in a horse-drawn cart for supplies, handling the job alone no matter what the weather conditions. Young "Charlie" had little interest in formal education, though his father helped start the community's first local school, but when he wasn't hunting, trapping, obtaining supplies, or working around the farm, he did learn to read. Maintaining his interest in reform politics, his father brought home the St. Cloud *Democrat* and other newpapers. In the 1870s, the papers carried news about the Granger movement, which marked the beginnings of the organization of American farmers as an active political force.

By the time Charlie turned twenty-one, he was bright, somewhat politicized, and finally ready for formal education. The family decided he would enroll at an academy near Sauk Center, from which he graduated after a year. Following a brief stint working for the Great Northern Railroad, Charlie gained admission into the reputable program in law at the University of Michigan. Growing serious about a career, young Lindbergh began to sign his papers with the initials "C. A." rather than the less formal Charlie. In March 1883, at age twenty-four, he completed the two required six-month courses and left Ann Arbor with a Bachelor of Law degree.

The young attorney opened law practice in Little Falls, Minnesota, a thriving agricultural community on the main line of the Northern Pacific Railway, where rapids spiralled down the upper Mississippi River. Little Falls had a population of just under 2,000 when Lindbergh set up his practice. He established a reputation for honesty and prospered. He married and fathered two daughters, but in 1895 tragedy struck. His wife died after eight years of marriage. After her death, Lindbergh focused on his legal work and began profitable speculation in the booming Minnesota real estate market.

While living in a hotel in the commercial center of Little Falls in 1900, C. A. noticed an attractive young schoolteacher, also living at the hotel. The two began a courtship. Evangeline Land, the daughter of a prominent Detroit, Michigan, dentist, had been educated at an elite school for girls and, like Lindbergh, at the University of Michigan, from which she graduated in 1899 with a degree in chemistry. Employed through an agency to teach school in Little Falls, Evangeline stayed on the job only four months before walking out over a dispute with the school principal about the location of her classroom and laboratory. She accepted Lindbergh's marriage proposal even though he was seventeen years older than she. On March 27, 1901, the couple wed at her parents' Detroit home.

Less than eleven months after their marriage, on February 4, 1902, the couple's only child, christened Charles Augustus, was born. C. A. Lindbergh built a house on the west bank of the Mississippi River and there the couple lived with C. A.'s daughters and their young son for the next four years. In the summer of 1905, however, the frame house exploded in flames and burned to the ground. Fire-fighters had failed to summon sufficient water pressure to reach the third floor, where the fire had ignited from an uncertain source. Although only three at the time, Charles vividly recalled being swept up in the night by a nurse and hustled out behind the barn, where he could only peer around the corner and watch as his home turned to ashes.

The fire symbolized the state of the Lindbergh marriage, which was also going up in smoke. The spark that had originally attracted young Charles's mother and father no longer bound them together. Realities had set in: C. A. was seventeen years older, a broad-humored, free-thinking westerner, whereas Evangeline was more refined in her tastes, sensitive about appearances and criticism, never entirely comfortable in Minnesota. The distances between them grew.

Charles could not fail to feel the strain between his parents. The tension only mounted when the fire forced the family to move to Minneapolis for the winter. Charles hated living in the city and missed the open land and tall trees on the 110-acre family farm. He also weathered a bout of measles that winter. He was glad to leave the city the next summer when the Lindberghs returned to Little Falls and lived in a hotel while their new, ten-room home was being built. (Donated to the state of Minnesota in

1931, the Lindbergh farm, with the second home preserved, is now the Charles A. Lindbergh State Park and historic site.)

In later years, Lindbergh insisted that his mother and father had continued to feel affection for one another, but their marriage, for all practical purposes, ended in 1906. C. A. and Evangeline rejected the option of divorce, however, which would have caused a scandal sufficient to abort Lindbergh's nascent political career. Although Lindbergh would never fully acknowledge it, the breakdown of his parents' marriage scarred him for life.

C. A. Lindbergh's reputation for scrupulous honesty and integrity had prompted several of his clients and friends to urge him to make a bid for the congressional seat representing Minnesota's sixth district. Reluctant at first, he decided to make the race because he was convinced that the bulk of his constituency—Minnesota's farm families—bore an unfair burden. While they worked hard to produce the grain and livestock that helped feed much of the nation, they were frequently overwhelmed with debt, illiquidity, and high interest payments. They blamed banks, eastern corporations, and railroads for keeping farm prices depressed. All too often, particularly in the midst of the periodic "panics" of the times, debts accumulated to such an extent that banks foreclosed on personal property. C. A. empathized with the farmers, often lent them money, and gave free legal advice.

Like many others C. A. Lindbergh blamed bankers, creditors, and business moguls—particularly those representing eastern financial institutions—for the plight of American farmers. As a candidate, Lindbergh identified with the Progressive wing of the Republican Party, which promised to rein in the power of monied elites. President Theodore Roosevelt had swept to office on a progressive platform in the election of 1904, promising to curb corporate abuses, ensuring a "Square Deal" for everyone, business-men and farmers alike. Lindbergh left little doubt that he intended to be one of T. R.'s most loyal followers. One of his campaign flyers noted that C. A. stood for "the inter-ests of the masses as against the interests of the classes" and that he was "in accord with President Roosevelt on all the great issues that are before the American people to-day." In the fall of 1906, despite taking on an incumbent Democrat, Lindbergh won election to the House of Rep-resentatives by a solid margin.

Young Charles joined his father on December 2, 1907, for C. A.'s swearing-in ceremony in the Capitol. For the next decade, Charles and Evangeline traveled from Min-nesota for an extended visit with her family in Detroit be-fore making their way to Washington, where they spent winters, Lindbergh and his mother in a hotel, and C. A. in a separate year-round residence. Young Charles admired his father and thrilled at meeting President Roosevelt, future president William Howard Taft, and prominent congressmen.

Charles attended various private schools in Washington, but he disliked formal education and complained that his hotel residence was a "prison" in comparison with the wide-open Minnesota farm. Lindbergh did enjoy the mu-seum at the Smithsonian Institution and walks in Rock Creek Park. Though it would be a long time before Lind-bergh followed in the family tradition and took an interest in politics, he insisted years later that he "was deeply im-pressed by speeches my father made on the House floor. Sometimes I sat beside him when he made them."

Young Lindbergh, a farm boy and Minnesota outdoors-man, much preferred that life to the stultifying conditions in the nation's capital. Back home in the spring and sum-mer, the boy could hunt, fish, ride horses, swim naked across the Mississippi, construct a raft, sit in his treehouse, explore open spaces, and tinker around the farm. These were the pastimes on which he thrived. School was a terrible nuisance for him—and he for his teachers—since he rarely paid attention. Neither C. A. nor Evangeline embraced formal religion, although the family sometimes attended church in Washington for appearances' sake. Even then young Lindbergh resented such hypocrisy and made his views known. He had no interest in long sermons about some "alleged Creator." Like his father, young Charles was a religious skeptic and a Social Darwinist.

When free from the burdens of school and church—and he was a child who enjoyed a great deal of freedom—young Lindbergh was a whirlwind of activity. "In the usual good weather of a Minnesota summer," he later wrote, "I spent most of my time outdoors." Armed with a .22 rifle at age six, he became an expert marksman who practiced on virtually every living creature that made the mistake of lifting its head high enough to enter his sights. Before he was ten Charles was proficient with a veritable arsenal, including a pistol, a twelve-gauge shotgun, and even a saluting cannon.

There was always excitement to be found in the Minnesota countryside. In late spring loggers sent great felled trees rolling down the Mississippi, forming a spectacular sight. When the logging camps moved south near Little Falls, Charles and his friends would get in the chow line, for the lumberjacks were famous for feeding anyone who cared to line up. "The food was plain, but limitless," the famed aviator recalled years later. Although he would later be nicknamed "Slim," and indeed stayed trim throughout his life, Lindbergh was always a notoriously big eater.

Despite his parents' separation—or perhaps because of it—Lindbergh remained closely connected to both of them. When his father was home in the summer the two would hunt, fish, and explore the banks of the Mississippi together. In the summer of 1915 the two ventured north to survey the headwaters of that great river. It was a grand adventure for young Charles, traversing Chippewa country, touring lumber camps, and comporting himself in the wilderness like a man, though he was only a boy of thirteen.

Charles responded positively to C. A., who believed that children ought to pursue their own interests unfettered by parental authority. He treated his boy with respect and acted as if he were older than he actually was, never worrying that such an approach might entail risks. To teach young Charles to swim, for example, C. A. simply tossed the boy off the bank of the Mississippi and stood above, roaring with laughter, while the youth flailed at the brown water, barely staying afloat. Before much longer, however, the two were swimming the width of the great stream together, naked as the Chippewa C. A. had known in his youth. Though normally away during winter, Charles endured his share of Minnesota's notorious inclement weather. On one occasion the boy found himself caught in a blizzard and had to trudge some fifteen miles, tugging his pony behind him, in order to survive.

A turning point in Charles's young life came when C. A. returned home from Washington in the summer of 1912 driving a Model T Tourabout. The next year, at age eleven, Charles assumed command of the vehicle. Both C. A. and Evangeline tried their hand at the wheel, but Charles alone mastered the machine. Although tall for his age, he could barely see over the dash when he extended his feet to the pedals below. Such trivialities were of no concern to Charles, who also proved adept at making the frequent repairs and adjustments that "Maria," as the Lindberghs dubbed their new machine, required.

Maria excited Charles's fascination with science and technology. In addition to being an avid Minnesota outdoorsman, Lindbergh had a serious and even studious side, despite his contempt for formal education. He could spend hours tinkering with the carburetor, pondering Maria's mechanics, learning its quirks. Only he could convince Maria to run in the cold weather. Charles also learned to avoid getting bogged down in the lanes left rutted and muddy by the horses and sleds that had heretofore claimed the roadways for themselves.

C. A. had purchased Maria for its practical benefit and it was Charles's duty on myriad occasions to chauffeur his father as he stumped through the congressional district at reelection time. During C. A.'s speeches, Charles spent most of his time tuning Maria's engine, and tuning out his father's oratory, although it would become clear in later years that C. A.'s words did not escape him entirely. The elder Lindbergh's emergence as a progressive had coincided with arrival in Washington of Wisconsin's Robert La Follette, who organized the midwestern progressives into an effective voting bloc. Although he was neither a brilliant speaker nor a writer, Lindbergh worked hard and effectively to help La Follette shape the progressive wing of the Republican party.

C. A. maintained a growing library, pored over populist and progressive tracts, studied the nation's financial system, and sharpened his condemnation of the "money trust." He attacked the system that allowed bankers, who produced nothing, to reap profits from money lent out on the basis of partial reserves, while the "common man" paid interest on necessary loans at rates over which he had no control. C. A. stood firmly for the farmer and producer. He stated his views directly and with little thought about whether or not they would be politically palatable. It was one of many traits his son would share.

The elder Lindbergh sharply opposed the Federal Reserve System, established in 1913 to regulate the banking system. C. A. argued that the regulators would be bankers themselves and that the injustices that he perceived in the federal financial structure would continue. Clearly C. A.'s fiery brand of populist progressivism had begun to wane in favor of bureaucratic reform. Feeling he had served out his usefulness in the House, C. A. declined to seek reelection in 1916. However, with Charles again acting as chauffeur, the elder Lindbergh sought the Republican nomination to the U. S. Senate against the eventual winner—and later secretary of state under Calvin Coolidge—Frank B. Kellogg.

In addition to excoriating the Morgan banking house and the money trust, C. A. now added an antiwar theme to his campaign. Such a position was popular in 1916, as President Woodrow Wilson and most of the American people still sought to avoid involvement in Europe's bloody conflagration. Lindbergh lost his bid for the Senate seat, and rather badly at that, finishing fourth behind Kellogg, another Republican, and a Prohibitionist candidate.

The defeat signaled the political demise of C. A. Lindbergh and the progressive Republicans in national politics. He returned to Congress to finish his last term and spent all of his energy opposing the seemingly inexorable drift toward U.S. intervention in the Great War. U.S. involvement would be a terrible mistake and would detract from the domestic agenda, he insisted, adding that intervention was being encouraged by the money, transportation, and war industry "trusts" precisely because they stood to profit from it. As he had done in opposing the federal banking system, Lindbergh wrote a book defining his antiwar position. However, once the United States intervened in World War I in April 1917, many interpreted Lindbergh's opposition as unpatriotic. During his 1918 campaign for the Minnesota governorship, opponents hurled eggs at Lindbergh, hanged and burned him in effigy, and even fired shots in his direction. Charles witnessed much of the bitter campaign, which ended in another decisive primary defeat for his father.

The bitter controversy aroused by C. A. Lindbergh's antiwar campaign foreshadowed the response to his son's anti-interventionism on the eve of World War II. While Charles paid little attention to politics at the time, it became clear in later years that he shared his father's conviction that war brought out the worst in a society and should be avoided as long as neutrality was a reasonable option. C. A. campaigned once again for the U.S. Senate in 1923, but for all practical purposes the war had ended both his and the progressives' political viability.

In earlier years, C. A.'s opposition to U.S. meddling abroad had not extended to Panama, which the United States for all practical purposes had seized from Colombia in a 1903 coup in order to construct the trans-isthmian canal. As patriotic Americans with a growing interest in transportation and technology, the Lindbergh family followed the progress of the Panama Canal with rapt attention. To midwestern progressives like Lindbergh, the canal not only represented a grand achievement but also would offer competition to the transcontinental railroads, whose unchallenged power farmers resented. After touring the canal zone during its construction, C. A. encouraged Evangeline and Charles to embark on a visit of their own. They did so in 1913, cruising the Caribbean up to the canal zone. Young Charles looked on in fascination as the massive earth-moving machinery ripped out huge chunks of ground in the name of progress. The presence of armed American marines throughout the canal zone also made a profound impression on the young man.

The Caribbean voyage with Evangeline typified a childhood where Charles remained in the close company of his mother. Except for the summers, when C. A. took time to be with his son, Charles spent most of his time with Evangeline. Charles relished the stints in Detroit, where he enjoyed the company of Evangeline's family, and especially of Grandfather Land. Not merely a dentist but a crafts-man credited with developing the first porcelain crown, Land spent hours in his laboratory entertaining his grand-son. In subsequent years Lindbergh often said that he never met a man more skilled with his hands. Charles nurtured his interests in science, craftsmanship, and tin-kering under Grandfather Land's influence. Like the elder Lindbergh, Grandfather Land was a Social Darwinist and religious skeptic.

When not in Washington or Detroit Charles and his mother lived together on the farm. Normally, they did quite well in C. A.'s absence. The only disruption in their tranquility was a serious one, however, as on several occa-sions mother and son were stunned to find bullets flying in their direction. Whether the random shooting incidents stemmed from C. A.'s political views was never learned, but they always occurred when the elder Lindbergh was away from the farm. Charles recalled one occasion that involved "a bullet whizzing past our heads as my mother and I were standing on the north side of our house." In another incident, while rafting on the river near his home, Lindbergh found bullets ripping into the water next to him. He calmly polled the raft ashore, raced home to get his own rifle, and—with a neighbor boy—canvassed the other side of the river until they spied the likely culprits carrying weapons. Taking careful aim, Lindbergh and his friend zinged bullets past the group, sending them dashing into the bushes. The sniping at his home never again occurred.

In calmer times Charles and his mother worked to-gether on the farm or, especially after the arrival of Maria, ventured out into the countryside. The youngster mar-veled at the speed with which the Model T traversed the rural Minnesota roads—faster than any horserider could ever have dreamed. These thoughts heightened the thrills Charles experienced when he contemplated the advance of technology. Years later Lindbergh recalled that "Maria gave us a freedom of travel we had never dreamed of before." He and Evangeline took advantage whenever they could to take a drive through the countryside. "Almost always we carried a picnic lunch, and when possible we found a lake shore on which to eat it."

The ease with which Charles and Evangeline traversed the Minnesota landscape inspired them in the summer and fall of 1916 to take an audacious road trip to the California coast. At age fourteen Lindbergh went west of Minnesota for the first time, doing all of the driving himself, to California and back. Maria, by this time, had been traded in for a more modern roadster, a six-cylinder "Saxon Six." Mother and son experienced every kind of weather, all types of travel conditions, and several breakdowns. Rutted and washed-out roads plagued the entire trip. Lindbergh recalled "rainy days in Missouri when mud collected on the Saxon's wheels until we could not move." After the forty-day trip to California, Evangeline decided to settle at Redondo Beach, where Charles enrolled in school. As usual, he displayed little interest and preferred to pass his time combing the beaches, indulging his lifelong fascination with nature and the sea. By the time they drove back to Minnesota, Charles had developed valuable confidence in his ability to conquer long distances—and do all the driving himself.

American entry in World War I in the spring of 1917 changed the lives of virtually all of the nation's residents. Unlike the elder Lindbergh, Charles and Evangeline expressed a certain pride in their nation's emergence as a world power, and they meant to do their part to support it. Much to Charles's delight, wartime conditions meant that boys who worked on farms could be excused from school to produce staples needed for the war effort. Charles, now fifteen and "fascinated with the idea of farming," took charge of the Lindbergh farm. He rose before dawn to care for the sheep, heifers, ponies, hogs, dogs, and various farm fowl. Lindbergh pored over pamphlets on agricultural science and technology. "Of course," he recalled years later, "I would institute modern methods. I ordered a tractor, a gang plow, a disc harrow, and a seeder, and started repairing our cedar-post fences." He also bought and operated a new milking machine, supervised a hired hand, and helped his mother care for her own dying mother whom she had brought to the farm with Charles's help. At night Charles would lie down on a cot on the back porch, exhausted but fulfilled by his hard labor. Under heaps of quilts and wool blankets, he would look up at the clear black sky, pondering the constellations, before dropping off to sleep.

Charles returned to high school only once, to claim credit for his wartime work on the farm and to obtain his diploma in 1918. After remaining at home another year, Lindbergh assented to his parents' decision that he enroll in college. By this time he motored everywhere on his latest passion, an Excelsior motorcycle. In the fall of 1920 Lindbergh rode off on his bike to Madison, where he intended to study mechanical engineering at the University of Wisconsin. Omnipresent, Evangeline would live with her son in Madison, where she had taken a school teaching job.

Lindbergh clearly had the aptitude to study at the university level, but remained put off by formal schooling. Furthermore, his parents had allowed him such freedom, and he had already assumed such responsibility—managing the family farm, driving across the country—that he could not abide childish rules and regulations by which the university governed student behavior. Moreover, the extracurricular activities that preoccupied most college students—dating, sports, parties, drinking, smoking—did nothing for Lindbergh. Accordingly, he spent most of his time tinkering with the Excelsior, or racing around Madison.

The daredevil in Lindbergh emerged on one occasion when he bet some friends that he could race full speed down a hill on the Excelsior and make a hairpin turn at the bottom. Instead of making it, Lindbergh slammed into a wire fence. His friends raced down the hill to check on him, only to find Lindbergh bloody with scrapes but calm, shaking his head and musing that if only he'd gunned the engine on the turn he would have made it. To their amazement, he picked up the motorcycle, made his way back up the hill, roared down it again, and gunned the Excelsior into the turn. Lindbergh made it this time and his friends now found him with the soon-to-be-famous boyish grin across his face.

The only aspect of university life that interested Lindbergh was the Army Reserve Officer Training Corps (ROTC), which he joined in his freshman year. ROTC drills involved use of weapons, in which Lindbergh excelled, and he quickly became a star of the campus rifle and pistol teams. After his freshman year he went to artillery camp at Camp Knox (now Fort Knox), Kentucky. After completing the regimen in rural Kentucky, Lindbergh took the Excelsior on another road trip, this time riding all the way to Florida and back.

Charles returned for his sophomore year at Madison, but failed to survive the second semester. Already on academic probation, Lindbergh had neglected his studies to such an extent that he headed for certain expulsion. Moreover, he had already made up his mind that he wanted to do something that the University of Wisconsin could not help him with. Charles Lindbergh had decided that he wanted to fly airplanes.

Lindbergh's interest in aviation flowed naturally from his fascination with science, technology, and advances in transportation. During the war he been enraptured by accounts of the flying aces, especially the American Eddie Rickenbacker, whose aerial dogfights had become legendary. Already a skilled automobile driver and motorcycle rider, Lindbergh decided to learn to fly. A career in aviation would allow him the opportunity to do the things he valued most in life—use his skills, avail himself of modern technology, and seek adventure. "I was glad I had failed my college courses," he recalled, fearing that otherwise he would have gotten a degree and taken a boring factory job.

Neither of Lindbergh's parents was happy about his decision, but both supported their son. Evangeline told Charles it was important that he pursue his own dream, but privately his decision to leave Madison devastated her. With Charles gone, Evangeline saw no reason to remain in Madison and decided to return to her family in Detroit. The separation of mother and son for the first time was a relief to Charles, who had begun to feel smothered by Evangeline's omnipresence.

Charles had learned about a company in Nebraska that would teach a prospective buyer of an aircraft how to fly. He mailed in the $500 fee required by the Nebraska Aircraft Company and rode off to Lincoln. The Nebraska Aircraft Company turned out to be something less than the operation its brochures had suggested. There was, in fact, no school as such in Lincoln, but Charles—or "Slim," as the lanky, six-foot-three-inch Lindbergh was quickly dubbed by the pilots, mechanics, and hangers-on at the airfield—did have the opportunity to learn about airplanes. On April 9, 1922, Lindbergh made his first flight, but the man charged with training Slim often failed to show up for the promised lessons. Lindbergh soon learned that his would-be mentor had lost his enthusiasm for the air after a close friend died in a crash. It was common knowledge that flying was a hazardous business and Lindbergh heard myriad stories about sensational crashes and fiery descents that ended in tragedy.

Slim remained undaunted, even after witnessing the death of two men who perished when a wing broke off their plane as they flew a loop over the airfield. He recalled an incident on the Minnesota farm when a plowshare had snapped loose and the disk went hurtling by his head. Lindbergh surely would have been killed had the missile been launched on a slightly altered trajectory. That incident, and other brushes with harm during his adventurous youth, had convinced Lindbergh that death could come at any time and one should make the most of life rather than shying away from its inevitable dangers.

Lindbergh went up with the pilots in Lincoln whenever he got the chance. The experience of flying so enraptured him that the dangers scarcely crossed his mind. "My early flying seemed an experience beyond mortality," he later recalled. "There was the earth spreading out below me, a planet where I had lived but from which I had astonishingly risen."

When he came back to earth Lindbergh asked questions, studied manuals, and watched mechanics take apart and reassemble airplane engines. The breakthrough for Lindbergh came when he convinced Erold Bahl, an aerial barnstormer, that he should become his assistant. Bahl, like a number of aviators in the early twenties, made his living by flying over country fairs and other local events. The war had called attention to aviation and people throughout the country thrilled to aerial stunts.

In May and June 1922 Lindbergh joined Bahl as he barnstormed across Nebraska, Kansas, and Colorado. Lindbergh displayed his skills as a mechanic and handyman, prompting Bahl to offer to pay all of Slim's expenses. Lindbergh even revealed his potential as a promoter, convincing Bahl that he would achieve an even greater response from the crowds if he allowed Slim to venture out between the wings of the biplane. Bahl consented and Lindbergh—wearing no parachute (most planes were not yet equipped with them)—edged his way onto the wing and began his brief career as a "wing-walker." He stood between the wings of the biplane, and waved to the thrilled crowds below.

Back in Lincoln at the end of the tour with Bahl, Lindbergh, running out of cash, worked odd jobs, but still spent much of his time at the airfield. There he met another aviator, Charles Hardin, whose wife Kathryn performed wing-walking and other aerial stunts. The Hardins also introduced Lindbergh to the parachute, and Slim stood mesmerized on the day he saw Hardin fling himself from the plane 2,000 feet above the airfield. "By stitches, cloth and cord," he later wrote, a man could make himself "a god of the sky for those immortal moments."

Of course, Lindbergh had to try it himself. When he approached Hardin with his request, however, Lindbergh blurted that he would like to try a "double-jump" in which he would activate first one chute, release it, and then activate a second. Hardin, anxious to promote and sell parachutes, agreed to Slim's request. After all, if this eager novice could perform a double-jump, it would reinforce his argument about the safety of parachuting. Lindbergh went up with Hardin, crawled out onto the wing, hooked himself onto a strut until he received the signal, then lowered himself over the side and was gone. Lindbergh activated his first chute, and cut it away with his Bowie knife, but a string had broken on the second chute and only the rush of the wind prompted its release, as Slim hurtled toward the ground.

Following this thrilling experience, Lindbergh bought a parachute of his own and joined another barnstormer, H. J. Lynch. Together Lynch and "Daredevil Lindbergh," as the advance posters called him, went on a tour across Nebraska, Kansas, Montana, and Wyoming that featured wing-walking and parachute jumping. A dog named Booster traveled with the aerial show and spent most of the time sitting on Slim's lap.

Although Lindbergh found these experiences exhilarating, being a daredevil was only a means of gaining the experience required to buy his own plane and fly solo. When the onset of winter ended his tour with Lynch, Lindbergh convinced his father to co-sign for a $900 loan that allowed him to purchase his own plane. World War I spurred airplane construction, but most had been built in Europe and the relatively few in the United States—just over 1,200 planes—were government surplus warplanes, cheaply constructed from wood and fabric, and with limited weight-carrying capacity. In the spring of 1923, Lindbergh purchased a 90-horsepower Curtiss JN 4D—a biplane known as a "Jenny"—for $500 in Souther Field, Georgia.

After purchasing the aircraft, Slim spent a few nights sleeping at the airfield until his new purchase was made ready for flight. Having had little previous experience with a Jenny, Lindbergh got off to a rough start, aborting his first takeoff and bouncing to a skidding halt. Another pilot helped him practice takeoffs and landings, however, and on a calm spring day, just before dusk, Charles Lindbergh lifted off and soared 4,500 feet above the tiny speck of an airfield he had left behind. At last his dream had come true: He was flying solo.

2

Wings of Destiny

Having achieved his initial goal of learning to fly, Lindbergh devoted the next several years of his life to becoming an expert aviator. Ultimately, he sought to advance the cause of American and world aviation. Courageous to a point that some considered reckless, Lindbergh willingly risked his life in behalf of that cause. Showing implacable determination, the young aviator allowed few obstacles to stand in his way.

After perfecting takeoffs and landings with his Jenny airplane in Georgia, Lindbergh, low on cash, set off in May 1923 on a barnstorming tour. He flew across Alabama and into Mississippi, where for two weeks he set down near Maben, a town teeming with aviation enthusiasts. Charging $5 a head, Lindbergh gave rides to some sixty customers, many of whom had heard about but never seen an aircraft, at least not at close range. After exhausting the demand around Maben, he spent the spring and summer flying across the South and Midwest, enduring all sorts of weather and surviving a variety of mishaps. The Jenny was so weak on takeoffs—especially on those occasions when a heavyset person occupied the passenger seat—that Lindbergh sometimes barely cleared the treetops. On one occasion, his plane veered slightly before takeoff as he bounced down a narrow street in a small Texas town. As a result, one of his wings clipped a telephone pole, prompting the Jenny to spin out and crash through a hardware store window. Slim volunteered to pay the damages, but the proprietor refused, noting that the entertainment of Lindbergh's visit to the small town had been worth the cost.

Minor mishaps and periodic near misses never shook Lindbergh's faith in his own abilities as a pilot. He even accepted an offer issued in Boulder, Colorado, of $1,000 to any pilot who could land his plane on the St. Vrain glacier. Lindbergh insisted he could carry out the stunt, intended to publicize the natural beauty of the Rocky Mountain foothills. Even if he wrecked the Jenny on his landing, Slim reasoned, he could buy a better plane with the $1,000 reward. When the promoters of the stunt reconsidered, withdrawing the offer as too risky, Lindbergh expressed disappointment.

Savoring the pleasure of flying over the family farm, seeing it whole for the first time, Slim returned to Minnesota in order to fly his father around in his last campaign. C. A. endured his first flight in tight-lipped silence and went on to suffer a humiliating defeat in the 1923 U. S. Senate primary campaign. Not only was C. A.'s political career over, but the family also soon learned that the elder Lindbergh suffered from a brain tumor. C. A. Lindbergh died in 1924, requesting a cremation. Ten years later, Lindbergh emptied his father's ashes out of his plane while flying over the family farm in Minnesota.

By 1924 Slim Lindbergh had already accumulated a substantial number of hours in the air. Now a veteran pilot, he became frustrated with the Jenny's lack of speed and power. Other aviators advised Slim to join the Army Air Service, which would enable him to fly more powerful planes such as the De Havilland 4B, or DH, which reached a top speed of 125 miles per hour compared to the Jenny's 75. The idea of joining the Air Corps appealed to Lindbergh's patriotism as well as his desire for more powerful wings. At the time army aviator Billy Mitchell was trumpeting the future of air power and displaying its military potential by staging mock aerial bombardments of ships. On March 19, 1924, Lindbergh, at the age of twenty-two, became one of 104 young men to enter the Army Air Service school at Brooks Field in San Antonio, Texas.

Slim loved flying fully as much as he hated formal education. He reacted with shock and dismay when informed that he would have to study at "ground school" to make the grade at the army air school. After receiving a low score on his first test, Lindbergh, for the first time, summoned the will to apply himself to a program of classroom learning. "I began studying as I'd never studied before," he recalled. The young aviator found himself cramming on "evenings, weekends, sometimes in the washroom after bed check far into the night." All the work paid off. Lindbergh survived the weeding out and went on to receive advanced training.

Slim graduated at the top of his class. He received his commission as a second lieutenant in the Army Air Force Reserve in March 1925, but not before surviving a midair crash that would have proven fatal had it occurred the previous year. Only nine days before graduation, Lindbergh's Army SE–5 fighter plane collided with another as they flew in a nine-plane gunnery formation. Both he and the pilot of the other craft bailed out and parachuted to safety, but the experience was harrowing. As his plane spun out of control, Lindbergh recalled years later in *The Spirit of St. Louis*, "Wires were howling; wooden members snapping; my cockpit had tipped toward the vertical. Our planes were revolving like a windmill." Slim barely got out alive. "I pushed past the damaged wing, hooked my heels on the cowling, and kicked backward into space."

At the time the young aviators joked about the incident, which earned them membership in the "Caterpillar

Club," so named for the insects from which their silk parachutes were made. More soberly, they reflected on their good fortune. It was the first year in which parachutes had been included as standard equipment during training flights. Lindbergh wrote a formal report on the mishap and published an account in an army newsletter, displaying for the first time his skills as a stylist. He sold a more dramatic version to the *New York Evening World*, capitalizing on the public's fascination with the promise—and dangers—of air power.

The accumulated air hours, drills, and classroom knowledge gained in the army air school made Lindbergh one of the most capable young pilots in the country. He returned briefly to stunts, taking a job flying passengers on tours and buzzing fairs and exhibitions with a company called the Mile-Hi Airways and Flying Circus in Denver. While performing such feats as flying at midnight over a fair with roman candles attached to his plane's wings, Lindbergh waited for something both more remunerative and meaningful than stunt flying or crop dusting. He found what he was looking for after returning in 1926 to Lambert Field in St. Louis, the nascent center of aviation in the Midwest.

Brothers Bill and Frank Robertson, acquaintances of Lindbergh, had responded to federal legislation allowing private air companies rights to carry the U. S. mail. The Robertsons hired Lindbergh as chief pilot to establish their route carrying the mails between Chicago and St. Louis. The job offered Slim everything he wanted: adventure, excitement, danger, and the opportunity to prove the value of aviation. Lindbergh also enjoyed living in St. Louis, which gave him an opportunity to enlist in the Missouri National Guard. "Slim" Lindbergh had now become "Captain" Lindbergh.

Lindbergh planned the mail route with his usual thorough attention to detail. He mapped out the 285-mile route between St. Louis and Chicago, using the Chicago and Alton Railroad to mark his route. He identified nine fields near farms along the way where he could make an emergency landing and telephone call if forced down. The mail flights proceeded smoothly through the first summer, but in September Lindbergh ran into heavy fog that precluded him from landing in Chicago. Worse still, without informing their chief pilot the Robertsons had removed a 110-gallon fuel tank from his De Havilland to repair a leak, replacing it with an 85-gallon tank. Suddenly, Lindbergh's engine shut down as he searched in vain for a break in the fog. He had no alternative but to bail out, whereupon he endured a surreal and terrifying descent.

"Since I thought it was completely out of gasoline," he later explained in *The Spirit of St. Louis*, "I had neglected to cut the switches before I jumped. When the nose dropped, due to the loss of weight of my body in the tail, some additional fuel apparently drained forward into the carburetor, sending the plane off on a solo flight of its own." As Lindbergh descended in his parachute, the plane went down with him, threatening to mow down its own pilot as he floated helplessly in his chute. The noise of the engine would fade away into the fog, only to become audible again as the circling plane returned to Lindbergh. Fortunately, the plane circled just outside of Lindbergh's path of descent. He landed safely in a cornfield amid stalks that stood high over his head. The aviator found his way to a farmhouse where he encountered a farmer who had heard the crash and was incredulous to find the pilot in one piece. Together they found the plane and recovered the U.S. mail, which was soon retrieved and sent on by rail.

Lindbergh and the two pilots who worked for him shepherded the mail through the bitter winters common to the American Midwest. Their planes were buffeted by high winds, rain, sleet, ice, and hail. In early November 1926, as Lindbergh left Springfield for Peoria on his normal route, he encountered a late fall blizzard that forced him to look for an early landing. Finding none even after flying close to the ground and dropping flares, the aviator climbed back to 13,000 feet and bailed out in a horrendous gale, which caused an "excessive oscillation which continued for about five minutes and could not be checked." Rocked in the night sky in his parachute, Lindbergh endured another terrifying descent that culminated, appropriately, with him plowing through a barbed-wire fence.

The young pilot had now earned the distinction of becoming the first U.S. flyer to have made four emergency jumps from his plane. Once again, the mailbags were found intact, although the aircraft was, again, demolished. Lindbergh had now been at the helm when the Robertsons lost half their fleet, but neither accident had been Slim's fault and the owners never tried to blame him.

At age twenty-four Lindbergh was almost routinely risking his life as a part of a widespread effort to establish commercial aviation in America. His life was an obsessive pursuit of conquest of the air. Even on days off from the mail route Lindbergh would fly private passengers to supplement his income.

Lindbergh's obsession with aviation reflected what historian Joseph J. Corn has called the "winged gospel." Lindbergh and other aviation pioneers used such terms as "miraculous" and "wondrous" to describe their early flying experiences. Flying constituted a sort of "technological religion" in which its practitioners "worshiped the airplane as a mechanical god and expected it to usher in a dazzling future, a virtual millennium." The advance of aviation inspired a mystical faith that progress could overcome problems that had plagued humanity for centuries. Flying was thus Lindbergh's life and religion. He never doubted that his efforts put him on the cutting edge of a revolutionary advance in scientific technology and human affairs.

With the stakes so high and the dangers ubiquitous, Lindbergh believed it was incumbent on him to live a clean life. He had sampled but rejected alcohol and tobacco, which he concluded were unhealthy and therefore senseless. If not uninterested in women, Lindbergh had certainly decided that they were far from a priority at the time. Absence of a social life and pressures of the job probably contributed to Lindbergh's notorious penchant for practical joking. For years he pulled brutal pranks such as placing reptiles in his fellow pilots' beds; substituting kerosene for water in their drinking jugs; and pouring ice-cold water in the faces of sleeping aviators.

In contrast to the terrifying excitements experienced in the air, Lindbergh could become bored on routine mail flights. He spent those times daydreaming about the future of aviation and contemplating the variety of feats that were regularly being performed as aviation came of age. Since the first flight on December 17, 1903, by Orville and Wilbur Wright at Kitty Hawk, North Carolina—a flight that went 120 feet and lasted 12 seconds—aviators had been trying to outdo their predecessors. By World War I the public, much of which had dismissed talk of flying machines as fairy tales, followed the progress of aviation in the war. In the postwar period the public devoted rapt attention to air disasters, barnstorming feats, and, increasingly, long-distance flights. In 1923 two army pilots gained fame by completing the first flight across the continental United States.

Lindbergh did not attempt to be the first flyer to cross the Atlantic. Successful transoceanic flight began with crossings by lighter-than-air dirigibles. In 1919 three U.S. Navy seaplanes left New York and one arrived at its destination in Plymouth, England. Another flight that year from Newfoundland to Ireland earned a $50,000 prize even though the pilots landed ignominiously in an Irish bog. In 1926 the public celebrated the flight of Richard Byrd and Floyd Bennett across the North Pole. Attention next focused on a New York-to-Paris flight, which had only then become technically feasible as a result of improvements in aircraft engines.

When Lindbergh began flying the mail, the New York-to-Paris route was the most talked-about challenge in world aviation. If one could carry enough fuel, Lindbergh thought to himself as he soared over midwestern cornfields, the 3,400-mile flight might easily be accomplished. Considering what he had already experienced, Lindbergh reasoned that a trans-Atlantic flight "couldn't be more dangerous or the weather worse than the night mail in winter." Moreover, aviation technology had resulted in the production of new aircraft that would simplify the task. The new Wright-Bellanca, an ultra-light single-winged monoplane, was just the sort of craft that could accomplish the feat.

Though he was only twenty-five years old when he began planning a trans-Atlantic flight, Lindbergh had been flying four years and had amassed almost 2,000 air miles. He rated his skills highly and concluded that he could make the New York-to-Paris flight that others, far more famous than he, had failed to achieve. Lindbergh read every account he could find of the failed initiative led by French aviator René Fonck, whose Sikorsky had crashed on take-off in Sepember 1926. Fonck and his copilot scrambled free, but two other crew members burned to death in the wreckage. Their failure left the Orteig Prize, a $25,000 offer from a Frenchman who operated hotels in New York, up for grabs.

While Lindbergh always mourned any tragedy involving fellow aviators, he criticized Fonck's approach. The Frenchman had loaded down the powerful Sikorsky with a crew of four and all sorts of what Slim considered superfluous baggage, including leather upholstery and even a bed.

Lindbergh concluded that a successful New York-to-Paris flight would be accomplished in a much lighter, single-engine plane. Indeed, he thought the crossing could be accomplished by a single man. He intended to be the one to prove it.

Obsessed with the mission, Lindbergh made plans with characteristic single-minded intensity. "I'll now bend every thought and effort toward one objective—landing at Paris," he thought to himself. "All else is secondary." Lindbergh carefully wrote down all the benefits of making the flight himself: he could promote not only the cause of aviation, but also put America first in the race to Paris. If successful—and Lindbergh expected no other result—his flight would call attention to St. Louis as a center of aviation. He gave little thought to failure, it seems, although he did decide to take along a rubber raft in case he was forced down.

As Lindbergh began to formulate his plans, he realized a fundraising campaign would be required to purchase the appropriate aircraft to accomplish the solo flight. After Lindbergh explained his plans to a group of St. Louis businessmen, they gave him a $15,000 check in support of the initiative. Next, Lindbergh wrote to aircraft builders about constructing a single-engine plane, but the major manufacturers—Fokker, Wright, Travel Air, and Columbia—rejected him. Most considered the idea of a solo flight, with no one to relieve the pilot over the Atlantic, little short of insane. Finally, however, Lindbergh achieved a breakthrough with a small San Diego company, Ryan Aircraft, which agreed to build the plane he had in mind.

Lindbergh had stopped flying his mail route in 1926 and decided to move to San Diego to supervise the construction of the aircraft. He joined the engineers and craftspeople at Ryan as they worked doggedly on the project they all hoped would make history. Although they made rapid progress in the spring of 1927, it appeared that Lindbergh and his group would lose the Orteig Prize before they got off the ground. New missions were already beyond the stage of preparation and ready for flight. Lindbergh began poring over maps of the Pacific in preparation for selecting an alternative flight into aviation history, but he put them aside when tragedy after tragedy struck down his Atlantic competitors. The culmination came in early May, when two French aviators left Le Bourget Aerodrome in Paris, but never arrived in New York. By this time, Lindbergh himself was ready.

On May 10, 1927, aware that other flight plans were nearing the takeoff stage, Lindbergh boarded his craft—christened *The Spirit of St. Louis* in honor of the city and his financial backers—and made a record-shattering flight over the Rockies from San Diego to St. Louis. Eschewing plans for ceremonies in his home city, Lindbergh ate a quick meal, met his supporters, and boarded *The Spirit of St. Louis* again for a seven-hour flight to New York. The little plane with a massive fuel tank in front of the pilot handled beautifully on its cross-country trek. Lindbergh felt ready to challenge the Atlantic.

At this point the young aviator became nationally known. He welcomed publicity for St. Louis and the cause of aviation, but what would become a characteristic distrust of the news media emerged during the waiting period in New York. On the day he arrived in the city, reporters crowded onto the airfield. Lindbergh, who once had seen a man killed by an airplane propeller, was sure that it would happen again as jostling reporters rushed toward his plane. After a practice run, a crowd of photographers forced Lindbergh to veer off his landing path, causing damage to his tail skid. The photographers did not even receive a reprimand. Adding to the insult, reporters wrote that Lindbergh had damaged his plane by coming in too fast on his landing! It seemed to Slim that reporters went wherever they wanted and wrote whatever they wanted. They called him the "Flyin' Fool"—a nickname he despised—emphasized the dangers of his flight, and embellished the tragedies that had befallen other aviators. "Accuracy, I've learned, is secondary to circulation," Lindbergh complained.

What angered Lindbergh most about the press, however, was its harassment of his mother. Although he would talk endlessly about aviation, Slim refused to answer incessant questions about his family or personal life. Undaunted, reporters located Evangeline and peppered her with questions. Did she know how dangerous her son's flight would be? Was she aware of all the aviators who had been killed attempting to cross the Atlantic? Emphasis on the dangers of the flight prompted Evangeline to make a hasty journey from Detroit to New York. Lindbergh reassured his mother but he did not want her in the city as he made his last-minute preparations. She returned to Detroit feeling somewhat comforted, but the aviator's contempt for the press remained.

In mid-May *The Spirit of St. Louis* was ready and so was Lindbergh. Two of his competitors, however, had also lodged their aircraft at Long Island's Roosevelt Field in anticipation of a New York-to-Paris flight. The only delay in flight plans was a stormy weather front over the Atlantic. While Lindbergh waited for the weather to clear, he went over last-minute preparations and went on modest tours of the city. Already, however, it was becoming difficult for him to go out in public. Although he had tried to appear incognito, a passerby at Coney Island had blurted "There's Lindbergh!," forcing the flyer and his entourage to flee. On the evening of May 19, Lindbergh planned to attend the theater but only after arrangements were made for him to sit backstage, out of public view.

Before the play even began, however, the weather bureau reported the breakup of the storm front over the Atlantic. That was all Lindbergh needed to hear. He abandoned plans for the theater, grabbed a quick dinner, had an aide pick up five sandwiches "to go," and returned to his hotel for a nap. Slim had been able to catch sleep under almost every imaginable circumstance and would have done so even on that historic occasion, but for a nervous body-guard stationed outside his door. Just as Lindbergh was dropping off, the excited guard opened the door and blurted, "Slim, what am I going to do when you're gone?" Lindbergh tossed and turned for another hour, then gave up and went down to his hangar at Roosevelt Field. He was pleased to see no activity in the hangars of his rivals.

At dawn the Lindbergh team made final preparations. The mechanic who revved *The Spirit of St. Louis* looked worried, however, explaining that in the cool, wet New York weather the plane's engine was turning over a few revolutions short of full power. The aircraft, loaded down with fuel, would be carrying 5,250 pounds—about 1,000 pounds more than it had ever weighed before. Would Lindbergh be able to get the aircraft to lift off the rain-soaked runway, or would it go down in flames as Fonck's plane had done on the very same field? The decision was Lindbergh's. The feel of the plane during test flights had convinced him that *The Spirit of St. Louis* would lift off despite the heavy load, but no one could be sure. Neither could anyone say what effect the rain-softened runway would have on his efforts to lift off. "In the last analysis," Lindbergh recalled, "when the margin is close, when all the known factors have been considered, after equations have produced their final lifeless numbers, one measures a field with an eye, and checks the answer beyond the con-scious mind." To those who knew him, the decision Lind-bergh made came as no surprise.

The aviator checked his charts, compass, and the crude periscope required to look ahead because the main fuel tank obstructed a direct frontal view. He tucked away his sandwiches and water, checked the plane's instruments, and signaled that he was ready to go. As some 500 people looked on, Lindbergh fastened his safety belt, pulled goggles down over his eyes, put in his earplugs, and, with several men pushing on the wing struts to help get underway, *The Spirit of St. Louis* began its long rumble toward destiny. The plane, feeling "more like an overloaded truck than an airplane," Lindbergh recalled, slowly picked up speed down the runway until he had it open at full throttle. "The halfway mark streaks past—seconds now to decide—close the throttle, or will I get off? The wrong decision means a crash—probably in flames." Lindbergh had passed the point of no return. His plane, spewing water from puddles along the way, lifted off, only to have the wheels touch down again. At last, after another light bounce—the entire plane now trembling from the strain on the engine—Lindbergh pulled the craft off the ground. Patiently he nosed the airplane forward, clearing a set of telephone wires by twenty feet. The time was 7:54 A.M. It was May 20, 1927. He had been awake for twenty-three hours.

Lindbergh had decided to fly a great-circle route, taking advantage of the curvature of the earth to reduce distance and flying time. He flew across the Long Island coast, then out over thirty-five miles of open sea to the Connecticut shore. He had never flown over that much open water before, but had to smile ruefully when he contemplated what lay ahead. After crossing Connecticut and Massachusetts, Lindbergh left the American coastline behind for the endless horizon of open sea. The aviator pondered his own "arrogance in attempting such a flight. I'm giving up a continent and heading out to sea in the most fragile vehicle ever devised by man." Lindbergh could not have felt more alone, but that was precisely when he was at his best. No reporters, no entourage, no copilot and crew to be responsible for, only Lindbergh and his aircraft, or *We,* as he later named his first book on the historic flight.

Once out to sea, Lindbergh grew weary and longed for sleep, even though he was less than a tenth of the way to

Paris! He thought of his plane, burning off its fuel, functioning just as he and the engineers in San Diego had planned, and grew angry with himself for even thinking of rest. "I must stay alert," he told himself, "and match quality of plane and engine with quality of piloting and navigation." He was hungry, too, but Lindbergh eschewed ingesting food that might increase his desire for sleep. The aviator lifted his plane higher off the ground—he had been flying just above the breaking waves below—and exposed his head to fresh air in order to revive himself.

Without sextant, radio, or even a direct view ahead because of his plane's unique construction, Lindbergh wound his way across the Atlantic by dead reckoning. The flyer passed the first test of navigation when he located the green shoreline of Nova Scotia through the fog. As he passed over land and headed out to sea, the aviator inevitably began to play over all of his own mishaps and aviation disasters he had witnessed or heard about. He began to question the merits of a life raft, which offered a chance of survival if forced down at sea, instead of a parachute. He had declined to carry both because of the extra weight.

Hungry, deprived of sleep, and confined in his wicker chair, Lindbergh was alone in a flying cocoon. But it was his own—no one else had ever flown *The Spirit of St. Louis*—and his moments of fear and grim calculation were interspersed with bursts of exhilaration. Although he had an entire night and day still ahead of him, the desire for sleep was sometimes overwhelming. He closed one eye, then the other, then both, but only for a second at a time. He stamped his feet, diverted water and rushing air into his eyes, and squirmed in his seat, but felt himself losing a deadly struggle. "My whole body argues dully that nothing, nothing life can attain, is quite so desirable as sleep. My mind is losing resolution and control." He recalled the long night trudging through the snow during his youth in Minnesota, when he had stopped to rest in a snowbank. He knew then, as now, that he must rise and carry on or face certain death.

Lindbergh varied his routine and played different scenarios through his mind to remain alert. He flew at high altitude, then low; used his left hand, then his right; sat up straight, slouched back; thought about disaster, then victory. He spent long stretches of time imagining what he would do in the event his engine gave out. Could he land on the great white cakes of ice he now saw floating in the North Atlantic below? He could make a fire, but how long could he live in the cold on five sandwiches? Every hour he took fuel and instrument readings, recording them in his log.

After eleven hours Lindbergh averaged just about 100 miles an hour, which, if all went well, would put him in Paris with plenty of fuel to spare. Deciding that he would risk expending a little fuel for a final gesture toward humanity, Lindbergh buzzed the tiny town of St. John's on the Newfoundland coast, drawing the attention of boaters and fishermen below. Ahead lay 2,000 miles of open sea— and the longest night of Lindbergh's life.

As daylight receded Lindbergh encountered stormy weather. He almost welcomed the call for concentration and planning, which took his mind away from sleep deprivation. The aviator climbed to 10,500 feet, hoping to endure an occasional thunderhead rather than being buffeted by the body of the storms below. At that altitude, however, Lindbergh began to feel the chill and a pilot's sixth sense informed him of danger. Ice! Everywhere the beam of his flashlight shone, he saw a black sky filled with "countless, horizontal, threadlike streaks." Ice clung to the wings of his plane and slowed his progress. "I'll have to fly around these thunderheads," Lindbergh thought. "But can I? There are more masses ahead, and fewer stars. Will they merge into one great citadel of storm?"

He considered turning back. It was still not too late to retrace his steps across Newfoundland, Nova Scotia, and back to Long Island. But in the time it would take to do that, he could be flying over Ireland. And if only he found Ireland, Paris would follow. Lindbergh pressed on, now wide awake with the tension. Gradually the storm clouds lessened, stars appeared, and the moon floated into view above the North Atlantic sky. Soon he was closer to Ireland than to New York.

The dawn. If only he could keep himself alert until light returned to the sky. Lindbergh fought to keep his plane on course, repeating to himself that the only alternative was "failure and death, failure and death." But the incessant demand for sleep returned with a vengeance. The aviator sang, squirmed, and forcibly held his eyelids open. He succumbed on a few occasions, but only for a moment at a time because of the unique construction of *The Spirit of St. Louis*. It was a remarkably sensitive aircraft, even more so as it became lighter from burning fuel, and wavered noticeably in the absence of a firm hand. The buffeting of the plane would begin as soon as Lindbergh dozed off, jarring him from the edge of sleep time and again.

At the halfway point Lindbergh had planned a celebration—a sandwich and some water—but instead he pressed on into the night, begging for dawn. "Sometimes the hands of the clock stand still. Sometimes they leap ahead a quarter-hour at a glance. . . . Then, on the thousandth or two thousandth time I'm levelling out my wings and bringing the nose back onto course, I realize that it's day." Lindbergh now descended toward the sea, his ears popping, until he levelled out and looked down at great breakers backed by gale winds. "It's a fierce, unfriendly sea—a sea that would batter the largest ocean liner." While Lindbergh knew he had little chance of survival if forced down in such a sea, he realized at the same time that he had been riding a tailwind across the Atlantic through the night. That being the case, Lindbergh concluded that he might well be ahead of schedule.

For most of the day Lindbergh bore his way through great banks of fog, experiencing the sensation of sleep with his eyes open, living "on the borderline of life and the great realm beyond." Dancing between the human and spirit worlds, Lindbergh no longer bothered to keep his log, resigned himself to accept whatever fate dealt him, but always pressed on in what he hoped must be, what had to be, the direction of Ireland. When he broke out of the fog bank and into blue sky, modest white caps on the green sea below, Lindbergh calculated he might be only a few hours from the Irish coast. After more than twenty-six hours in the air, the sighting of a porpoise—a living creature!—exhilarated the pilot. "I feel that I've safely recrossed the bridge to life, broken the strands which have been tugging me toward the universe beyond."

Soon after, the aviator spotted a flock of seagulls: How far away could land be? In any case, with his aircraft now bereft of much of its fuel, he would be bouyant if forced down on calmer seas closer to land. The odds had shifted in Lindbergh's favor. Even if something went wrong, he at least stood a good chance to live. In the twenty-seventh hour an even happier sight appeared: a tiny black speck that soon became a boat . . . surrounded by other boats. Lindbergh buzzed them in his excitement, but got no response from the men on board. Not wishing to waste precious daylight, he gave up and flew on. Where was the *land?*

At last, twenty-eight hours after he left New York, Lindbergh spied the unmistakable contour of a large land mass. After checking and rechecking, the charts confirmed the astonishing fact that he was virtually dead on the course he laid out one day in San Diego. "The southern tip of Ireland! On course; over two hours ahead of schedule; the sun still well up in the sky; the weather clearing!" The need for sleep and the phantom voices were gone. Lindbergh had seen human beings and villages below. Time was "no longer endless, or the horizon destitute of hope." Paris lay 600 miles to the southeast.

In a moment of giddiness Lindbergh considered flying over Paris, dipping his wings, and soaring on to Rome, another seven hours on his circle route, and over 4,300 miles from New York. Why carry all the gasoline and not use it? he reasoned. But by the time he reached the French coast, Lindbergh had determined that he would focus his attention on finding Le Bourget Field. As he sped toward his destiny the aviator realized he had no visa. Would he be admitted to the country? Would anyone even be there to witness the end of the longest nonstop air flight in history?

By the time Lindbergh arrived over Paris, darkness had long since fallen. He circled cautiously, looking for the airport on the northeast side of the city. He passed by the lighted field once. After finding no other, he concluded that the site he had seen so close to a city factory and swarming with automobile traffic must be Le Bourget. He had no way of knowing that it was the reports of his sighting—over Ireland, England, and Normandy—that had brought the automobile traffic to Le Bourget. At 10:24 P.M. European time on May 21, 1927, Lindbergh set down *The Sprit of St. Louis* and rolled into the blackness in the center of Le Bourget. Thankful that he encountered no obstructions, the young American aviator turned his plane to taxi toward the floodlights and hangars, but had time only to cut the engine before mobs of screaming people engulfed his plane.

Lindbergh had done it; he had conquered the Atlantic. The irony was that after flying solo longer than any human being before him, Lindbergh would soon find it virtually impossible ever to be so alone again.

3

The Hero

Lindbergh's reception on the ground in Paris was a harbinger of the life he would lead as an international celebrity. Crowds of people swarmed the young aviator. Totally unprepared for the frenzied public response, Lindbergh would struggle the rest of his life to accommodate himself to his new status as popular hero.

When he arrived at Le Bourget on the historic evening of May 21, the situation was hopeless. Aware that the aviator had been sighted en route to Paris, police and soldiers had tried to erect barricades around Le Bourget. Tens of thousands of Parisians, and those who had driven into the city from the countryside, ignored the obstacles. They converged on the airport and tore through steel fences surrounding the field. As Lindbergh eased *The Spirit of St. Louis* to a stop, they climbed onto his plane, ripping off souvenirs and causing substantial but reparable damage. Lindbergh tried to ask for a mechanic to guard his plane, but got no response. He was left pleading, "Does anybody here speak English?"

Oblivious to Lindbergh's concerns, the ecstatic crowd hauled the exhausted pilot out of his plane and passed him over their heads, filling the air with a thunderous roar of celebration. Despite having landed his plane, Lindbergh remained airborne. He had visions of falling into the crowd and being trampled to death, but soon landed on his feet. Fortunately, a souvenir hunter plucked the aviator's cap off his head and put it on. "There is Lindbergh!" someone shouted, pointing toward the man who now wore Lindbergh's hat. The crowd swung toward the man with the hat and away from the hero. The incident allowed Lindbergh to lower his head and make his way with two French pilots to their automobile. They drove to a hangar where the aviator met Myron T. Herrick, the U.S. ambassador to France, who took charge of the hero's welcome.

Lindbergh himself seems to have had one thing on his mind: not sleep, not food, not even his own heroics. Rather, the aviator could think of nothing beyond the fate of *The Spirit of St. Louis,* which he had last seen being ripped apart by the crowd. The pilot insisted on being taken back to his plane, which he was sure by now had been destroyed. In fact, French officials had taken the plane to a hangar for repairs, which they hoped to complete before Lindbergh could see the damage. In addition to the gaping holes torn in the fuselage, someone had stolen the aviator's logbook. It was never recovered. "It was a great shock to me" to see the damaged plane, Lindbergh recalled.

After seeing his plane, and confirming through his own inspection that the damage could be repaired, Lindbergh accepted Herrick's invitation to stay at the U.S. Embassy. Donning a pair of the ambassador's pajamas, the young aviator enjoyed a steak dinner. By prior arrangement, for which he had been paid, Lindbergh then gave an exclusive half-hour interview to *The New York Times* before meeting with other reporters. The pilot described the flight, telling of his battles with fatigue, but noting that he had landed with enough fuel to fly another thousand miles. The aviator insisted that he himself could have summoned the energy to have flown "half as far again." The normally restrained *Times* featured a three-deck banner headline and devoted most of its first five pages to Lindbergh's flight. Newspapers around the country reacted in similar fashion.

Not until 4:15 A.M. in Paris—sixty-three hours since his last sleep—was Lindbergh shown to a bed. He awoke at noon the next day to chants of "*Vive* Lindbergh" emanating from the courtyard outside the embassy. Although one might have expected resentment or at least a measure of reserve on the part of the French, whose pilots had perished over the Atlantic trying to achieve Lindbergh's feat, in fact the enthusiastic reception continued throughout his stay in France. "Captain Lindbergh" expressed his sincere admiration for the lost French fliers and declared that they had had to contend with headwinds whereas his own flight, backed by tailwinds, had been "easy." He also met with the mother of one of the deceased pilots, expressing his sorrow and admiration for her son's courage.

Ambassador Herrick, determined to improve Franco-American relations that had grown sour over World War I debts and other issues, called Lindbergh the ideal American hero. "Had we searched all of America," Herrick wired President Calvin Coolidge, "we could not have found a better type than young Lindbergh to represent the spirit and high purpose of our people." Tall, handsome, and plainspoken, Lindbergh made a strong impression. Over the next few days he picked up the Cross of the Légion d'Honneur from the French president, addressed the French Assembly, and toured Napoleon's tomb, always comporting himself with grace and humility. Lindbergh, Herrick later explained, had brought "the spirit of America in a manner in which it could never be brought in a diplomatic sack."

On May 28 Lindbergh boarded his patched-up aircraft, flew over Place de la Concorde, and waved good-bye to the Parisians. After flying to Brussels for another celebration, the aviator went on to London for a meeting with King George V. After a prolonged briefing on protocol before royalty, Lindbergh found himself more nervous about meeting the king than he had been confronting the Atlantic. The monarch quickly put him at ease, however, with his first question. "How did you pee?" the king wanted to know. Lindbergh explained that he had taken along an aluminum can for that purpose. The aviator met other members of the royal family, placed a wreath on the tomb of Britain's unknown soldier, and once again served as an effective ambassador of America's overseas image.

Not satisfied with his trans-Atlantic feat, Lindbergh had planned to fly around the world. He had informed Herrick of plans to fly over Europe and Asia, and return to the United States through Alaska. President Coolidge vetoed Lindbergh's plans, however, making clear that the American people would not be content to allow the Europeans a monopoly on celebrating their hero. The pilot must come home, Coolidge declared, and dispatched a naval vessel to retrieve Lindbergh and his airplane.

On its arrival in Chesapeake Bay, four destroyers, two army balloons, and forty aircraft met Lindbergh's ship, the *Memphis*. Evangeline, with whom Lindbergh had spoken by special trans-Atlantic telephone hook-up from Paris, had been summoned to the Executive Mansion (the White House was being refurbished at the time), where she had dined with President and Mrs. Coolidge. When the *Memphis* arrived on June 11, Evangeline was taken out into the harbor to welcome her son home. They spent a half hour together in Lindbergh's cabin before coming ashore.

The warm reception in Europe had made a profound impression on Lindbergh, but it could not compare with what followed in the United States. Officials escorted the aviator on a long processional culminating at the Washington

Monument. There the president, ambassadors, congressmen, and other dignitaries greeted him while a massive
crowd extended as far as the eye could see. In a brief
speech Coolidge declared that Lindbergh's was "the same
story of valor and victory by a son of the people that shines
through every page of American history." The aviator himself said a few words, which the crowd greeted with thunderous applause and tears of joy. The president then pinned
the Distinguished Flying Cross, the first ever awarded, on
Lindbergh's chest. Stunned by the display of mass emo-
tions, Lindbergh was left wondering "if I deserve all this."

The ensuing four-day celebration in New York made
the reception in Washington seem minor by comparison.
To honor the aviator the stock market shut down, hotels
were filled, and an estimated 3 or 4 million people
jammed the streets for a ticker tape parade that exceeded
the 1918 armistice celebration. Tons of confetti rained
down on the Minnesota farmboy turned national hero.
Lindbergh would never forget the exhilarating experience
when, or so it seemed, all of Manhattan stopped to honor
his accomplishment.

On leaving New York, Lindbergh flew to St. Louis and
circled the city so that the people there could have a good
look at "their" plane. After celebrating with his financial
backers, Lindbergh traveled to Dayton, Ohio, for a meeting with Orville Wright. The visit, a sincere gesture to
honor one of the pioneers of American aviation, also won
Lindbergh praise from the press and public. A huge throng
gathered outside during Lindbergh's visit and began to
close in on Wright's home. The crowd dispersed only after
Lindbergh responded to appeals, going out on a balcony
to acknowledge them.

The American public remained in a celebratory mood.
Politicians, public figures, newspapers, and magazines
trumpeted Lindbergh's—and America's—achievement.

Radio, which began commercial broadcasting in the United States in 1920, had blossomed into a major industry. An estimated 30 to 50 million people listened to Lindbergh's Washington address over the airwaves. Radio commentators, now heard all over the country over the new National Broadcasting Company network, kept Lindbergh's achievement at the center of public attention. He was great copy. Newspaper and magazine circulation soared as a result of stories on Lindbergh. A new magazine, *Time,* named Lindbergh its first "Man of the Year" in 1927. More than 200 homespun poems poured into *The New York Times*. Throughout the country people wrote letters, telegrams, poetry, essays, editorials, and sermons on the meaning of the flight. The emotional response reflected the unprecedented scope and intensity of the celebration. Advertisers competed to buy time to sponsor special programs on the aviator, his background and first flying experiences, the construction of *The Spirit of St. Louis,* and the evolution of his trans-Atlantic flight.

Lindbergh's achievement affected the American people on an emotional level. The aviator, as the *Washington Post* put it, received "that frenzied acclaim which comes from the depths of the people." The intensity of the celebration shocked Lindbergh and those who contemplated it. While he had been first to fly from New York to Paris, others after all had flown the Atlantic and even received more prize money. As *The New York Times* observed, "There has been no complete and satisfactory explanation for the enthusiasm and acclaim for Captain Lindbergh."

Explaining the tumultuous reception accorded Lindbergh has been a challenge for historians, too. Part of the explanation is to be found in the character of American society in the 1920s. While many Americans remained impoverished, the twenties were a decade of unparalleled prosperity. Expanding industries, such as the automobile, spurred production in other sectors of the economy, including the steel, glass, and rubber industries. Most Americans could find jobs, had more money to spend than ever before, and enjoyed increased leisure time. Advertising flourished, with the help of the radio, as producers attempted to appeal to consumers nationwide.

The emergence of a national media made Americans hungry for heroes like Lindbergh, whose exploits transcended the mundane. Lindbergh was hardly alone, however. With spectator sports increasingly popular, Americans celebrated Babe Ruth, a left-handed slugger for the New York Yankees who clubbed a record sixty home runs the year of Lindbergh's flight. Like Lindbergh, Ruth captured the imagination of the public for an unmatched individual achievement.

Even more popular were the movie stars who capitalized on the dramatic appeal of motion pictures. Beginning first with silent films, attendance skyrocketed until by 1930 about 100 million Americans went every week to the movies, which featured screen stars such as Charlie Chaplin, Douglas Fairbanks, and Gloria Swanson.

Lindbergh's flight was not the only event to garner prolonged media exposure in the 1920s. The press followed various fads, crazes, and stunts, including flagpole sitting and marathon dancing. Most riveting of all, however, was a tragic incident in which a Kentucky cave explorer, Floyd Collins, found himself trapped belowground. For two weeks in 1925 thousands of people drove their automobiles to the site in rural Kentucky and reporters kept a breathless national public apprised of ongoing efforts aimed at freeing the trapped explorer from his underground crypt. The efforts failed and the nation mourned Collins's death.

The rapid social changes that accompanied the new prosperity and modernization of American society unsettled many Americans. Protestant evangelists Billy Sunday and

Aimee Semple McPherson achieved a wide following in their call for a revival of Christian fundamentalism as a refuge amid the rapid changes of American society. The 1925 Scopes "monkey trial" in Dayton, Tennessee, over the teaching of evolution in public schools, reflected similar anxieties. Revival of the Ku Klux Klan and a circus atmosphere surrounding the trial and execution of two Italian immigrants, Nicola Sacco and Bartolomeo Vanzetti, attested to the twenties' racial and nativist anxieties.

Spiritual emptiness beneath a veneer of material prosperity was a leading theme of American literary figures, including F. Scott Fitzgerald, Eugene O'Neill, Sinclair Lewis, and John Dos Passos. They described a society that failed to achieve its ideals, that drank and gambled illegally, and generally fell short of its moral pretensions.

Public enthusiasm for popular diversions, heroes, and celebrities stemmed in part from lingering disillusionment over World War I. Although the Allies won, the war had hardly served to usher in a "new diplomacy" or make the world "safe for democracy," as President Woodrow Wilson had inspired people to believe that it would. Instead the conflict left the United States bitterly divided over its future role in the world, as reflected in the prolonged debate and ultimate rejection of the Versailles Treaty and the League of Nations. The postwar Red Scare brought to the surface tensions within American society.

The United States suffered from a sense of moral loss in the postwar period. The high idealism of the great crusade to make the world safe for democracy had given way to disillusionment. Widespread violation of the Prohibition law fostered cynicism and contempt for government. In this climate, the nation venerated heroes and sought causes to champion. Lindbergh's flight was a source of regeneration. The public grasped the opportunity it offered as a symbol of national renewal.

Lindbergh offered the unambiguous victory that the public craved. He had promised to conquer the Atlantic, and he had delivered. Moreover, Lindbergh had harnessed the power of a machine to advance the cause of humanity, rather than to destroy it, as the weapons of the Great War had done. These accomplishments so impressed the American public that Lindbergh became a national hero.

The solo flight resonated with a public that had long celebrated individual achievement. Lindbergh had done on his own what other aviators working together had failed to accomplish. He had acted decisively—a necessary ingredient for heroism—deciding on his own to depart the moment he heard the weather was clear. A slick runway and an overloaded plane, dangers that had already claimed the lives of others, did not impede his quest. He overcame cold, ice, fog, sleep deprivation, and lack of navigational equipment. The *Nation* called him "a young Lochinvar who suddenly came out of the West." His flight represented "the kind of stuff which the ancient Greeks would have worked into a myth."

Lindbergh's flight also echoed romantic themes from the American past. The press called him the "Lone Eagle," appropriating the symbol of national greatness and of soaring high above the crowd. Like the rugged individualists, self-made men, and frontier heroes of the American folklore tradition, he had set out into the unknown wilderness and returned as its master. Commentators drew frequent comparisons between Lindbergh and Daniel Boone and Davy Crockett, frontiersmen who had also ventured alone into the unknown, combating hostile forces, while advancing their country's glory in the process.

The solo flight ignited a nostalgia for the pre-industrial past, to a time when individual achievement could still make a difference: but it also represented an optimistic bridge to the future by calling attention to the accomplishment of the aircraft. In the face of an increasingly urban, mechanized society, Americans were reassured by Lindbergh's display of the ability to harness modern technology to good effect. While many feared that a war of unprecedented destruction and the fast pace of modern industrial society meant that the machine was overwhelming the individual, Lindbergh had shown that the two could live in harmony and achieve greatness.

Lindbergh's flight prompted a celebration of business and technology, as well as individual achievement. The aviator himself emphasized the role of technology, insisting that the flight was the culmination of twenty years of progress in aviation rather than the achievement of one man. President Coolidge, famous for the homily that "the business of America is business," agreed, declaring that "American genius and industry" had been Lindbergh's "silent partner" during the solo flight. "I am told that more than 100 separate companies furnished materials, parts or service" in construction of *The Spirit of St. Louis,* the president noted.

The final ingredient in explaining the sources of Lindbergh's heroism was the aviator himself. He was modest and clean-living. He came from an immigrant family and was close to his mother. These qualities offered a sharp contrast to a society that many associated with corruption, organized crime, intemperance, and declining moral values. Tall, handsome, and "girl-shy," Lindbergh embodied the innocent all-American boy. Throughout his life he flashed a classic ear-to-ear grin that became a well-known trademark. The young aviation pioneer could have destroyed the heroic image Americans so much wanted to embrace had he displayed arrogance or greed in capitalizing on his fame. Instead, Lindbergh resonated an "aw, shucks" modesty when he discussed his dramatic achievement, continually credited the forerunners of American aviation, and the airplane itself. Lindbergh did not say "I" but rather "We," as he titled his account of the flight, thus giving equal credit to *The Spirit of St. Louis.* Lindbergh said what the public wanted to hear, and they idolized him for it.

Lindbergh did not covet fame—indeed, he would soon find it intolerable—but he did capitalize on it to promote the cause of aviation and make himself financially secure. The former motive clearly outweighed the latter. Although Lindbergh profited handsomely from his flight, he could have garnered much more wealth than he did. The aviator, of course, collected the $25,000 Orteig Prize and the same sum from the Vacuum Oil Company, which made the fountain pen he had used in keeping his flight log. The series of articles on his flight that Lindbergh wrote for *The New York Times* earned him $60,000. These were large sums of money in the 1920s and, combined with other earnings, made him a wealthy man.

The monetary value of the gifts and money *declined* by Lindbergh would have allowed him to amass a fortune of $5 million or more. For example, the aviator received 150,000 francs from a French aviation club, but returned the money with the proviso that it be divided among families of men who had died in aviation. He turned down an astounding offer of $1 million raised by a group of businessmen who declared that Lindbergh, now a national treasure, should no longer risk his life in flight. If Lindbergh would simply agree to give up flying, they would give him the money.

The Lone Eagle received from sources in 69 different countries more than 15,000 unsolicited gifts, some of which—like a modern touring car from the Franklin Motor Company—were quite valuable. He gave away most of the gifts or had them put on display in museums in Washington and St. Louis. Hollywood besieged the aviation hero with various offers, including a $500,000 contract with William Randolph Hearst for a film on aviation, which Lindbergh turned down. Madison Avenue weighed in with various lucrative endorsement offers, but to little effect. Lindbergh also rejected an opportunity to make well over $100,000 by going on a speaking tour.

In addition to the series of newspaper articles, Lindbergh's contract with *The New York Times* had included provisions for a ghost-written book on his dramatic flight. When he read a draft copy of the manuscript, however, Lindbergh immediately regretted having signed the contract. He informed the *Times* that he felt uncomfortable with another man's words appearing under his name. With 100,000 orders already waiting to be filled, however, the *Times* was anxious to publish the book. Lindbergh's only alternative was to do the actual writing himself—and fast.

Lindbergh, who had received poor grades in the few English classes he had taken, now launched his career as a writer. As with most of his endeavors, he became successful at it. The Lone Eagle proceeded to amaze his publishers by holing up in the Long Island home of the wealthy Harry Guggenheim, a World War I navy aviator with whom Lindbergh had become friendly, and churning out the required 30,000-word account of his historic flight. While the end product, titled simply *We,* could not compare with his later literary efforts, the book was an instant and lasting best-seller that earned its author some $200,000.

Lindbergh's approach to fame was to exploit opportunities that built public support for commercial aviation. If he profited at the same time, so much the better. An example was his decision to embark in the summer of 1927 on a forty-eight-state tour in *The Spirit of St. Louis.* The venture proved a brilliant public relations triumph for the cause of aviation and garnered Lindbergh a substantial sum, although less than half of the $1 million he had been offered not to fly.

The idea for this tour originated with Guggenheim, who shared Lindbergh's desire to promote commercial aviation and who underwrote the venture. Lindbergh responded enthusiastically for he liked nothing more than to be airborne in *The Spirit of St. Louis*. But he insisted on two guaranteed conditions. First, "We must always be on time —if we have to get up in the middle of the night to do it. We want to show people that aviation can come through on time." Second, Lindbergh wanted assurance that crowds would be kept off the runways and away from his plane. The aviator had no desire to mar a visit by killing or injuring a bystander. Nor did he wish to repeat the harrowing experience that followed his landing at Le Bourget.

As was nearly always the case, Lindbergh's careful planning resulted in a successful tour. On only one occasion, during a serious thunderstorm, did Lindbergh fail to land *The Spirit of St. Louis* on time during the 22,350-mile journey that included 260 hours in the air. "I landed in every state in the union, spoke in scores of cities, dropped messages on still more," he recalled years later. "I inspected sites for airports, talked to engineers and politicians, and tried to convince everyone who would listen that aviation had a brilliant future, in which America should lead." Lindbergh also enjoyed himself, indulging in a few stunts, buzzing just above the treetops, and joining other pilots in formations.

Fame was irritating as well as rewarding, however. Several times Lindbergh had difficulty landing because the crowds awaiting his arrival had pushed out onto the runway. On at least one occasion he set down *The Spirit of St. Louis,* only to take off again as people poured onto the field. Once he had landed his plane, Lindbergh displayed little patience for the packs of reporters who invariably descended on him. He talked willingly about aviation, but the Lone Eagle never adjusted to his status as a celebrity by giving the reporters what they wanted: the lively quote, tales of aerial heroics, and, increasingly, information about his personal life.

Despite mounting tensions with reporters, Lindbergh's forty-eight-state tour achieved more than he and Guggenheim had thought possible. The aviator impressed crowds from coast to coast and won the admiration of influential Americans who might aid the cause of commercial aviation. One of these was Henry Ford, whom Lindbergh met when he flew *The Spirit of St. Louis* into Dearborn, Michigan. Ford's company had built Maria, Lindbergh's first car, but the auto magnate was notoriously suspicious of airplanes. Knowing this, Lindbergh invited Ford up in *The Spirit of St. Louis* purely as a matter of courtesy, expecting him to decline. To Lindbergh's surprise, Ford accepted and soon gazed below in fascination as they flew over his home and sprawling auto plant. Lindbergh's plane had, of course, been designed for solo flight, but Ford was too enraptured to complain about being "hunched up on the armrest of the pilot's seat." Captivated by his aerial tour, Ford began flying on a regular basis, although he trusted his life only to one pilot whom Lindbergh had recommended. Beyond his newfound personal attraction to flying, Ford had been sold on the future of aviation. Lindbergh thus played a central role in Ford's decision to begin airplane production at his Michigan plant. Lindbergh and Ford, both mavericks, found they shared much in common and forged a friendship that would prove crucial to Lindbergh later in his life.

By the end of the forty-eight-state tour, Lindbergh had achieved one of his major goals. He had received pledges raising millions of dollars for airport construction around the country. While the Lone Eagle was only one among many influential Americans promoting the development of commercial aviation facilities, the flight to Paris and the highly publicized forty-eight-state tour did more for the cause than anything else. In large measure as a result of Lindbergh's efforts, the number of airfields in the United States increased 72 percent from 1927 to 1930. Many of them were now illuminated to accommodate night time air traffic. The same three-year period produced an 80 percent increase in the amount of air mail carried. In 1929, before the stock market crash, the public had invested $400 million in aviation securities.

Lindbergh won favorable publicity and national recognition for his efforts. In November 1927 Coolidge pinned the National Geographic Society's Hubbard Gold Medal on the aviator's chest. The president credited Lindbergh, whom he called a "courageous, clear-headed, sure-handed youth," with advancing "aeronautic plans . . . far beyond any dreams of six months ago."

Lindbergh continued to work closely with Guggenheim and another wealthy benefactor who was to play an important role in his life, Dwight Morrow. Lindbergh met Morrow, a partner in the J. P. Morgan and Company banking house, in the course of the latter's investigation of military aviation, which followed the criticisms by the flamboyant army general Billy Mitchell. Courtmartialed for "insubordination and conduct unbecoming of an officer" in 1926 after unceasing criticism of the nation's military aviation program, Mitchell called for expanded air power and an autonomous air force. Appointed by Coolidge to investigate air power in the wake of the Mitchell imbroglio, Morrow had encouraged changes that culminated in the 1926 Air Corps Act upgrading military aviation, but not creating the separate force that Mitchell had advocated.

Following Lindbergh's historic flight, Morrow proved anxious to meet the young aviator and get his views on

American air power. Impressed by Lindbergh's innocence, Morrow and Guggenheim feared that the Lone Eagle might be exploited. They shared the young hero's desire to promote aviation and offered their advice on what promotional offers he might accept and refuse. Morrow also made Lindbergh a preferred client at the Morgan banking house, thereby allowing the aviator to buy securities at a discount, among other benefits. Impressed by Morrow's wealth and power, Lindbergh enjoyed the privileges offered him.

Lindbergh recognized that wealthy elites such as Morrow and Guggenheim could use their influence to promote aviation. He also enjoyed the company of these men, whom he respected as hardworking and successful individualists. What he perhaps appreciated most from his relationships with wealthy elites, however, was the insulation they afforded him from society at large. By taking advantage of opportunities to spend extended periods of time on the secluded estates of these prominent men, Lindbergh could escape from the reporters and crowds of people who constantly stalked him.

Following Morrow's service on the presidential commission on aviation, Coolidge named his former Amherst College classmate ambassador to Mexico. Intent on improving strained relations between the United States and Mexico, Morrow invited Lindbergh to make a goodwill tour to Mexico City. Lindbergh had already decided to make one final long-distance, nonstop flight before donating *The Spirit of St. Louis* to the Smithsonian Institution. He accepted Morrow's proposal and made plans to depart from Washington, D. C. Alarmed by the dangers of a 2,100-mile flight, Morrow advised Lindbergh to make the trip in stages, putting in public appearances along the way. But Lindbergh, more threatened by the public than the dangers of air travel, insisted on making the long solo flight.

On the eve of his 2,100-mile capital-to-capital flight, Lindbergh appeared before the House Appropriations Committee to lobby for aviation funding. He then accepted an invitation to appear before the entire House, where he was introduced as "America's favorite citizen." Each member of the House then filed past Lindbergh on the dais for an opportunity to shake the young aviator's hand. That same week both the House and the Senate voted unanimously to award him the nation's highest honor, the Congressional Medal of Honor. Lindbergh spent the rest of his time in Washington flying navy planes and preparing for his Mexican adventure.

The aviation hero embarked in *The Spirit of St. Louis* on December 13, 1927. This time he was well rested for a trip that would constitute about half of the distance he had flown to Paris. After arriving in the vicinity of Mexico City, Lindbergh spent considerable time flying low in an effort to identify a town or landmark on his map. Finally orienting himself in relation to Mexico City, he flew on to the capital, where Morrow and 150,000 anxious people awaited him. Since Lindbergh had shown himself to be notoriously punctual during the forty-eight-state tour, Morrow feared as the estimated time of arrival passed that the odds had finally caught up with the Lone Eagle. Had he gone down in his record-breaking plane somewhere over unfamiliar Mexican soil?

No one was more relieved than the U.S. ambassador when Lindbergh soared into view. He landed after more than twenty-seven hours in the air. Mexico's president, Plutarco Elías Calles, greeted the Lone Eagle, presented him with the keys to the city, and called for "closer spiritual and material relations" between the United States and Mexico. In Washington Coolidge reciprocated, declaring that Lindbergh's flight marked the opening of a new chapter in U.S.–Mexican relations. Over the next several days the Mexicans celebrated Lindbergh's latest achievement, establishing the aviator as perhaps the most popular *gringo* ever to have appeared in the Mexican capital. Lindbergh described his tour in another series of articles in *The New York Times* for $50,000.

Now more enamored than ever with Lindbergh, Morrow insisted that the aviator stay with his family in Mexico City through the Christmas holiday. Lindbergh's only concern was his mother, Evangeline, but the Morrows solved that by inviting her to join them. Also traveling south for the holiday were two of Morrow's three daughters, Elisabeth and Anne, students at Smith College. The latter, the bright and attractive middle daughter, soon began to confess her attraction for Lindbergh, but only to her diary. Both Anne, twenty-one at the time, and "Lindy," as the girls teasingly called him (since it made him cringe), were too shy to act on their mutual attraction. Anne actually spent more time with Evangeline, and the two quickly forged a close relationship based in large measure on their mutual love of Charles.

Lindbergh enjoyed his two-week stay in Mexico City, but he remained shy around women and the Morrow girls made him nervous. He made plans to escape on another aviation adventure. By now keenly interested in establishing a pan-American system of commercial aviation, Lindbergh left Mexico City for another goodwill tour. He flew down the Central American isthmus, across Colombia and Venezuela, up the Antilles to the Virgin Islands and Cuba, and finally back to St. Louis, which he considered home base.

Once again, Morrow and others expressed their concern about Lindbergh's decision to fly across the sea and into the unfamiliar skies over Latin America. The Lone Eagle himself seems to have had virtually no concern about his own safety, however. The risks merely enhanced the adventure.

As far as Lindbergh was concerned, life without risk was boring, indeed a fate worse than death. "A trip around the gulf and the Caribbean Sea," he decided, "would be an adventure worth another reasonable risk of life."

As usual, most of Lindbergh's problems on the tour centered around the huge crowds that gathered at his planned stops. As always, he managed to get through, accomplishing his mission of promoting the growth of aviation. At the same time, Lindbergh's presence increased respect for the United States and its accomplishments. He was thus a successful agent of American technological and cultural expansion. While flying over the Panama Canal, a long-time interest, Lindbergh took note of the proliferating number of American-built hotels and restaurants along the canal zone. "I sensed the power, the wealth, the accomplishment of my United States of America," he recalled.

After flying to St. Louis, Lindbergh planned a series of events in the spring of 1928 that he intended as a "farewell tour." He decided to culminate the tour in Washington, where he would present *The Spirit of St. Louis* as a gift to the Smithsonian Institution. Lindbergh would miss the plane, which he dearly loved, but he realized too that "an accident with *The Spirit of St. Louis* would have had a detrimental effect on aviation." There was no need to further tempt fate: like the pilot himself, the aircraft had already become a national treasure.

In Washington Lindbergh formally received the Congressional Medal of Honor in a ceremony with Coolidge on March 21, 1928. He thus became the first nonmilitary hero to receive the award. Lindbergh was then ready to move on to a life of flight, business ventures, marriage, and family. He declared that he was now ready to get "out of the hero business" and made it clear he expected the public to go along with his wishes.

If only it had been that easy.

4

Crime of the Century

Charles A. Lindbergh was the all-American boy: tall, handsome, and a heroic conqueror of new frontiers. He was not, however, much of a ladies' man. In his youth, Slim had always been more interested in guns, cars, and his motorcycle. Then came his obsession with aviation. Lindbergh recalled in his autobiography that he "had always taken for granted that someday I would marry and have a family of my own," but a combination of his shyness around women and his unwillingness to take the time to date found him, at age 26, the nation's most eligible bachelor.

If Lindbergh was still a virgin, which seems doubtful, it was only because he had declined myriad opportunities to pursue sexual liaisons. Barnstormers and military aviators were notorious for capitalizing on the allure aviation seemed to have for some women. Prostitutes, too, could be found in the vicinity of airfields. Whatever the extent of his sexual experiences, Lindbergh had not had a relationship and had no girlfriend.

Part of the reason for his mounting tension with the press was news accounts that either called attention to Lindbergh's apparent lack of interest in the opposite sex or "reported me engaged to at least a dozen women, several of whom I had never seen." It was not an unusual occurrence for women to make themselves available to the aviation hero, sometimes in quite direct terms. As a result of his fame and the ubiquitous press, however, he had little opportunity to be alone with a woman. "Girls were everywhere," he recalled in his posthumously published 1976 autobiography, "but it was hard to get to know them. . . . There was never a chance for me to take a girl quietly to a restaurant or theater."

Despite the obstacles, after his farewell tour in *The Spirit of St. Louis,* Lindbergh set about looking for a relationship much as he might plan one of his aviation adventures. He would list his priorities, calculate the costs and benefits, and make a prudent decision. He decided that he wanted to find a partner who had "good health, good form, good sight and hearing." Of course, she would also have to learn to fly.

Twenty-two-year-old Anne Morrow offered everything that Lindbergh desired. Dark-haired, petite, and attractive, Anne was also athletic, having played basketball at Smith College. She had enjoyed flying with Lindbergh when he took her and her sisters up during his stay in Mexico City. Lindbergh had actually spent more time with Anne's sister, Elisabeth, but in the months after leaving Mexico, he found himself thinking of Anne. He decided that he wanted to see her again. He did not know it at the time, but Anne was already infatuated with him and she had been jealous of the time he had spent with Elisabeth.

In the fall of 1928 Lindbergh telephoned the Morrow estate at Englewood, New Jersey, and invited Anne to go flying with him over Long Island. After she accepted, Lindbergh arranged to fly out of a Long Island horse pasture to avoid the inevitable "hullabaloo" and "silly stories" that would result from the couple being seen together in public. Anne enjoyed the flight and accepted Lindbergh's invitation for a "ground date" a few days later. They cruised through the New Jersey countryside in his Franklin sedan. "When it was over," Lindbergh recalled, "we were engaged to be married."

Not even Anne's parents, living at the time in Mexico, knew of the couple's plans for several weeks. Since tabloid journalists kept a close watch on Lindbergh, offered bribes to servants for information, and even attempted to steal mail, there was little hope of keeping the secret. Lindbergh, as always, resented the intrusion into his personal life. "I had found relationships with the press difficult before I had a fiancée," he recalled. "I found them next to impossible thereafter." Lindbergh used various means—false names over the telephone, circuitous routes, evasive driving—but the media pursuit was relentless.

By February 1929, with rumors swirling about Lindbergh and one of the Morrow daughters, the Morrows released a public statement announcing the engagement of Anne and Charles. The story, of course, was an instant sensation. Both were young, attractive, and adventurous. The glamorous and wealthy couple were as close to regal as was possible in a country without royalty. (Lindbergh once complained that he suffered constant intrusions like a member of a royal family, but without an entourage to insulate him from the press and public. On the other hand, he admitted, royalty had to be on good behavior at all times, "whereas I don't.")

The proposed marriage surprised many. After all, Lindbergh, son of a firebrand progressive who had excoriated the "money trust," would be marrying into the family whose vast wealth derived from Dwight Morrow's former partnership in the very banking house, J. P. Morgan and Company, that C. A. Lindbergh had condemned. Lindbergh himself took little, if any, notice of the irony of the situation.

Evangeline, who had enjoyed Anne's company during her visit to Mexico, promptly approved of her son's intentions. The Morrows also gave their blessing, although not without some reservations. They liked and respected Lindbergh, but harbored concerns about their Smith-educated daughter's plans to join Charles in a career of aviation. While Anne was an intellectual, Charles was a college dropout (albeit one who received an honorary degree from the University of Wisconsin in 1928). While the Morrow family talked Shakespeare and Greek mythology at the dinner table, Lindbergh lacked classical education.

Anne recognized the differences between her and Charles, yet she wanted to marry a man of action. Responding to a questionnaire about future plans at the end of her senior year in a private high school, she had written, "I want to marry a hero." She grew enamored with Charles watching his deft manipulation of the aircraft during a flight in Mexico. She appreciated as well his clean-cut, boyish looks, level-headed behavior, and the type of consideration for others that had prompted Lindbergh to visit Anne's brother who had suffered a nervous breakdown.

As the couple spent long hours getting to know one another better, Anne discovered that Charles possessed more depth than she had first thought. While not intellectual, at least not then, he did have ideas, and good ones, especially about aviation, science, and technology. Anne, who had decided to become a writer and published some of her poetry during her senior year at Smith, learned that Lindy himself dreamed of being a writer. Eventually, their marriage would forge a literary as well as an emotional bond.

Acting with the secrecy that the situation required, the Morrows invited several guests for what appeared to be a casual gathering at their New Jersey estate. When the guests arrived on May 27, 1929, they found Evangeline and the Morrow family making final preparations for the surprise wedding of Charles and Anne. A group of some two dozen witnessed the ceremony in front of a fireplace in the family parlor. After the wedding the newlyweds set off secretly (after Charles had arranged for a friend to dress like him and decoy reporters on an airborne wild-goose chase) for a yachting honeymoon along the Maine coast. While honeymooning on the yacht, the Lindberghs successfully avoided the press and public until Charles went ashore for supplies at York Harbor, Maine. There he was recognized and soon a press plane buzzed them from above while another boat pulled alongside the Lind-berghs' yacht, using a bullhorn to request their presence on deck for pictures. The couple resented the intrusion and refused to appear.

After the honeymoon, Lindbergh hoped to avoid public scrutiny so that he might focus his attention on the two things that now mattered to him most: family life and commercial aviation. After conferring with Dwight Mor-row and Harry Guggenheim, Lindbergh had affiliated with two major commercial airlines: Transcontinental Air Transport (TAT) and Pan American Airways. The latter had been formed by an ex-navy flyer and Yale science graduate, Juan Terry Trippe, who in 1923 had started one of the first commercial air services in the United States us-ing surplus navy planes. By the end of the twenties Trippe had expanded his airline to compete with the German air-line Lufthansa, which was trying to tap the Latin Ameri-can market. Within a few years Pan Am dominated the Americas. Serving as the top consultant, Lindbergh plot-ted and tested north–south air routes. He made the first official flight of Pan Am's new amphibious Sikorsky S-40, the *American Clipper,* at the time the largest transport plane built in the United States.

TAT, too, wanted Lindbergh's expertise, but most of all they wanted his name. In return for $250,000, 25,000 shares of common stock, and an executive position, in 1928 Lindbergh allowed TAT to market itself as the

"Lindbergh Line." The company became known as Transcontinental and Western Airlines, and ultimately Trans-World Airlines or TWA. On July 27, 1929, Lindbergh, joined by Anne as copilot, flew from Los Angeles to Winslow, Arizona, the first leg of the first transcontinental air route. The Lindberghs had joined Hollywood celebrities, including Douglas Fairbanks and Mary Pickford, in promoting the new airline, whose planes featured such novelties as upholstered seat cushions, curtained windows, and tray tables.

While Lindbergh willingly capitalized on his fame to promote aviation and his own commercial ventures, he still insisted that his private life should not be subjected to public scrutiny. Despite such protests, the press and public engulfed the Lindberghs whenever in public. Anne, a woman of genteel manners, shared her husband's aversion to public attention. When they were not crisscrossing the country on a survey or expedition, the Lindberghs secluded themselves in the Morrows' New York apartment or at the 56-acre Englewood estate, determined to remain out of public view.

The press resented the Lindberghs' exclusiveness. Even when appearing at a public function, they often refused photographers' requests to pose together. Charles had no respect for the intrusions of journalists. Even when friends and Anne's parents tried to explain it to them, the couple failed to understand that their avoidance of the press only made its representatives devise ways to become even more intrusive. The press hounded the couple unmercifully when it got the chance, offered bribes to servants and doormen, tapped telephones, and even sent reporters undercover to apply for jobs on the grounds of the Morrow estate.

Resentment between the press and the Lindberghs increased when the couple waited more than two weeks before announcing the birth of their first child, christened Charles Augustus, who was born on his mother's twenty-fourth birthday, June 22, 1930. Convinced that she would get no privacy at any hospital, Anne elected to bring in medical equipment and have the baby delivered at their New York apartment. When no announcement came, the tabloids printed rumors of birth defects. Finally, Lindbergh called a press conference, from which he excluded five newspapers that he said had printed irresponsible material. He issued a birth announcement and gave out a photograph taken by himself of a healthy blue-eyed baby.

In 1930, with the desire for privacy paramount in their minds, the Lindberghs purchased a 425-acre site in the Sourland Mountain area near Hopewell, in southern New Jersey. They commissioned construction of a whitewashed stone, two-and-a-half-story home under a slate roof. Beyond the clearing for the house, thick woods covered the area. A planned runway near the home would allow the couple to fly to New York in twenty minutes and return to seclusion the same day.

By the winter of 1932, the Lindberghs and their baby, Charles, Jr., had moved into the first home they could truly call their own. They still often spent the workweek at the Morrow estate in Englewood, but passed virtually every weekend at the home near Hopewell. Lindbergh could never have expected that his new home would become the scene of a wrenching tragedy, one that would torment the couple for the rest of their lives. That tragedy was the kidnapping and murder of their 20-month-old son.

The kidnapping occurred on March 1, 1932, after the baby had been fed and placed in a crib in his room by Betty Gow, a nursemaid who had come highly recommended. Also staying at the home were the butler, Oliver Whateley, and his wife Elsie, the cook and housekeeper. Lindbergh did not return home from his work at the airline offices in New York and a trip to the dentist until 8:25 in the evening. He and Anne ate before the fireplace. At one point Lindbergh heard a noise and turned to Anne, asking, "What's that?" They could not identify the sound but assumed it came from the kitchen and resumed their conversation.

After Anne went up to the bedroom, Charles took up a book in the library, and Betty Gow went to offer Charles, Jr., his customary evening snack. She went into the room, leaving the light off so as not to startle the child, reached into the crib and found it empty. Shocked at first, Gow concluded that Anne must have picked up her baby. "Why, no, I haven't had him," Anne responded. The two assumed that Charles had taken the baby down to the library, but when Betty burst into the room and asked him, Lindbergh responded, "No. Isn't he in his crib?"

Lindbergh bolted up to the bedroom, found the blankets still pinned to the mattress by safety pins, but the baby gone. He was the first to notice the envelope lying on the sill of the southeast window. Having the presence of mind to warn everyone not to touch the envelope, Lindbergh went swiftly into the bedroom, took his Springfield rifle from the closet, and paused for a moment to meet the eyes of his despairing wife, already pregnant with their second child. "Anne, they've stolen our baby!"

"Oh, God," was all she could say in response. Lindbergh waited another moment while Whateley followed his orders to call the local police. Surprised that the phone lines had not been severed, Lindbergh went out with his rifle. The aviator could hear little but the howling winter wind outside and had no visibility in the black night. Finding no activity outside, Lindbergh returned inside, called his friend and attorney Henry C. Breckinridge, and awaited the arrival of first the Hopewell police and then the New Jersey State Police.

The commander of the State Police, Colonel H. Norman Schwarzkopf (father of the leader of American forces in the 1991 Persian Gulf War), and Breckinridge would be

Lindbergh's closest confidants in the four-year ordeal that followed. After showing police to the baby's room, one of Schwarzkopf's aides opened the envelope to reveal a crudely written note from the kidnapper. It demanded "50000$" and warned against "making anyding public or for notify the police. The child is in gut (good) care." The barely literate note, like the next thirteen the kidnapper would send, displayed a symbol of two interlocking circles outlined in blue. A large red dot appeared in the inner oval formed by the linking of the two circles. The kidnapper advised Lindbergh to respond only to notes containing his "singnature."

Taking personal charge of the investigation from the outset, Lindbergh decided that cooperation in every conceivable way with the kidnapper was the best means of getting his son back. He now regretted his decision to call the police—expressly forbidden by the kidnap note—and discussed with Breckinridge and Schwarzkopf what their course of action should be. After a sleepless night, unable to eat anything, the Lindberghs received the press and even offered coffee and sandwiches. Their estate was inundated with more than 100 reporters and photographers. Headlines soon exploded all over American newspapers.

The kidnapping of the "Eaglet" from America's first couple was, until the 1963 assassination of President Kennedy, the most sensational crime of the twentieth century. News of the Lindbergh kidnapping increased newspaper circulation more than 300 percent. The event, though a terrible tragedy, diverted public attention from the ongoing economic crisis that had ravaged the country since the onset of the Great Depression in 1929.

On March 4 a second note scolded Lindbergh for contacting the police, and upped the ransom demand to $70,000 since the process would now require more time. "We will form you later were to deliver the money," the note said. "But we will note do so until the Police is out of the cace and the pappers are quite." Getting the "pappers" to be "quite" was, of course, impossible, but for once Lindbergh thought the press might be helpful in providing him means of communicating with the kidnapper. Anne gave the baby's daily diet to the press, asking that it be adhered to for the sake of the child's health as he had been suffering from a cold. Lindbergh released a statement making it clear that he intended to cooperate with the kidnapper. Their only concern was the safe return of their child, he wrote, promising that he would not seek "to injure in any way those concerned with the return of the child."

Meanwhile, amid the storm of media attention, a series of hoaxes began to unfold. Many assumed that the crime must have been committed by organized crime "gangs," much in the news in the last year of Prohibition. In New York a hood named Vincent "Mad Dog" Coll had challenged the supremacy of the Dutch Schultz gang, using kidnapping and ransom against Schultz and his allies. Kidnapping and occasional shoot-outs followed as the "snatch racket" gained notoriety. Contributing to the theory that gangs had kidnapped the Lindbergh baby was a pledge of gangster Al Capone, lodged in Chicago's Cook County Jail on charges of income tax evasion, that he could obtain the child's freedom, but only if he were released from jail.

Schwarzkopf and others doubted the responsibility of organized crime, however, pointing to the crudely written notes and the relatively small ransom demand. Lindbergh, after all, was worth at least a half million dollars and his wife's family much more. Furthermore, a crude, home-built ladder had been found twenty yards from the house, with a chisel lying nearby. A shattered rung on the ladder brought to Lindbergh's mind the sound he had heard that evening while sitting by the fire. A footprint in the snow had been discovered outside the window from which the baby was taken, but the excited police had failed to make a cast of the print before it was obliterated. Overall, police considered the crime somewhat sloppy in execution and likely not the work of criminal gangs.

In addition to generating a series of hoaxes and crackpot responses, the kidnapping aroused widespread sympathy for one of the nation's most celebrated couples. One of the most sympathetic was Dr. John Condon, a retired 71-year-old Bronx, New York, schoolteacher who considered Lindbergh a hero and all-American boy. To Condon the kidnapping was an attack not merely on the Lindberghs but against America itself. The crime moved Condon to pledge, in an offer published in the Bronx *Home-News,* to donate his life savings of $1,000 to act as a go-between for the kidnapper, if only the culprit would return the child to its parents. On March 9, much to his amazement, Condon received a note from the kidnapper accepting his offer to serve as an intermediary.

While clearly eccentric, Condon was well known in the Bronx for his community activism, energy, and patriotism. A lifetime sports enthusiast, he kept himself in good physical condition and impressed many with his kindly manner and friendly smile beneath a white mustache. Lindbergh had never heard of Condon but when informed over the telephone of the contents of the note, complete with the enjoined circle "singnature," he knew it came from the kidnapper. Lindbergh authorized Condon to act as his go-between and endorsed the elderly man's suggestion that his initials, J.F.C., be merged together into the code name "Jafsie." After receiving a telephone call from the kidnapper, "Jafsie" arranged to meet with him in a New York City cemetery.

Although Condon thought he might be risking his own life, he went to the cemetery while a driver waited in his

nearby car. There Condon saw a man, who promptly pan-
icked, vaulted over a fence, and fled down the street to
Van Cortlandt Park. Condon followed and found the
man, holding his coat collar up around his chin, and iden-
tifying himself only as "John." Condon tried to win the
man's confidence immediately, asking him to sit "as my
guest" on a park bench. Condon informed the kidnapper
that he had not brought the money and would do so only
when assured that the baby would be returned safely.
They agreed that "John" would send the baby's sleeping
suit to confirm that he was indeed the kidnapper. Condon
asked the heavily accented man, "Are you German?" but
John replied, "No, Scandinavian." Condon tried to get
the kidnapper to soften, asking him what his mother
would think of his crime. John admitted his mother
would "cry" if she knew, but insisted that he was only a
messenger for a larger gang. John then stunned Condon
by asking nervously, "Would I burn if the baby is dead?"
Condon responded sharply, asking about the baby's condition, but John insisted that there was no doubt that the
baby was alive and in good health.

Determined to handle the ransom on his own, Lindbergh sold stock and received numbered gold certificates
from the Morgan banking house. After hearing Condon's
account he reasoned that the kidnappers were adhering to
their pledges and, once they had been paid, could be
counted on to return Charles, Jr. Aware of the events, the
New York police insisted that they be informed of the
time and place of the exchange so that they could follow
and arrest the perpetrator. Lindbergh refused.

On Saturday, April 2, Lindbergh himself accompanied
Jafsie as they followed the kidnapper's latest directions to
the edge of St. Raymond's Cemetery in the Bronx. As
Condon peered into the dark and began walking, both he
and Lindbergh heard the heavily accented voice, "Hey,

Doctor. Over here." A figure rose from behind a gravestone. Based on their earlier meeting, Condon had decided that the kidnapper would be content with $50,000 rather than the second demand for $70,000. After a brief argument, John agreed to the $50,000 ransom, although, had John insisted, Condon was ready to hand over the additional $20,000. Neither Condon nor Lindbergh realized at the time that John's willingness to settle on the spot for a smaller ransom suggested that he was more than merely the gang messenger that he claimed to be. Otherwise, John would not have been able to accept $20,000 less than demanded without consulting his superiors.

John thanked the doctor, observing that he had handled his intermediary role well, and gave him a note that purported to explain where the baby could be picked up. John warned that the note should not be opened for eight hours. Condon rejoined Lindbergh. After a short time they decided to disregard John's orders and open the note, which stated that the baby could be found on a "boad" [boat] named *Nelly* near Elizabeth Island in the Rhode Island Sound off Martha's Vineyard. Lindbergh, ecstatic in the belief that his child would be freed as promised, already had a plane ready. He flew out the next morning, carrying a blanket for Charles, Jr., while the Coast Guard searched on the water below. Back at their New Jersey home that evening, Anne readied the crib and switched on the light in the baby's nursery.

After two days of exhaustive searching, it was clear that there was no "boad" named *Nelly* on the Rhode Island Sound. Jafsie placed frantic ads in the Bronx newspaper, but this time John did not respond. In the ensuing weeks Lindbergh continued to follow up various leads. On May 12 the aviation hero boarded a launch in the Chesapeake Bay to search for his son. Charles had received a tip from a Norfolk, Virginia, man who claimed that he had seen the Lindbergh baby in the hands of a gang. The man later admitted he had made up the entire tale. While on the launch, Lindbergh received the news of the discovery of his son's body. Schwarzkopf had already told Anne, who took the news with remarkable stoicism. The body of 20-month-old Charles Augustus Lindbergh, Jr., had been found by a traveler in a shallow ditch near the Princeton-Hopewell Road. The medical examiner later declared that he had been killed the night of the kidnapping.

Returning at once and driving to the Trenton morgue, Lindbergh asked the attendant to remove the cover that had been placed over the badly decomposed body. Calmly, he reached into the mouth and counted the child's teeth, then looked carefully at the boy's distinctive, upturned toes. Asked if he could confirm the baby's identity, Lindbergh replied, "I am perfectly satisfied that it is my child." He stayed to witness the cremation and later scattered the ashes from the air, as he had done with his father's remains.

The appalling murder of the Lindbergh baby outraged the public and created a climate conducive to reforms aimed at strengthening federal power to combat crime. In 1932 Congress passed the "Lindbergh law," which provided for federal criminal jurisdiction in cases involving kidnapping and ransom notes. President Herbert Hoover expressed some reluctance about extending federal authority but, perhaps in part because of his friendship with Lindbergh, signed the measure into law. The next president, Democrat Franklin D. Roosevelt, had no such reluctance and called for further efforts to bring "the Federal Government's anti-crime machinery up to date." The Bureau of Investigation under J. Edgar Hoover was strengthened and renamed the Federal Bureau of Investigation. These changes in federal law enforcement emerged from a climate of concern generated by the growth of organized crime during Prohibition and capped by the sensational Lindbergh case.

The public not only supported stronger federal authority to combat crime, but also looked for scapegoats to explain the failure to capture the kidnapper. Rumors, speculation, and wild charges abounded. Unfounded stories about crime gangs continued to circulate. Some insisted that Colonel Lindbergh's servants had plotted the kidnapping, others that Condon was behind the incident from the start. To combat the scurrilous charge against Condon, Lindbergh publicly thanked the doctor for his courage and assistance.

Colonel Schwarzkopf's State Police, which had primary jurisdiction over the case, received intense criticism. A graduate of the U.S. Military Academy at West Point, Schwarzkopf had been an artillery officer in World War I. Until the Lindbergh case no one had questioned the competence of a man so highly regarded that he had become head of the State Police in 1921 at the age of only 26. Lindbergh backed Schwarzkopf throughout the ordeal, although the State Police at the time was really a quasimilitary organization rather than a modern law enforcement agency trained in criminal investigation. Lacking facilities and equipment for a sophisticated probe, Schwarzkopf operated from a makeshift command post in Lindbergh's garage. With the exception of the handling of footprints outside the window, however, Schwarzkopf insisted that the State Police had handled the case as well as they could.

Pursuing the case relentlessly, Schwarzkopf focused his investigation on the Lindbergh servants, both at the home near Hopewell and the Morrow home in Englewood. There was some reason to suspect that the kidnapping had been, at least in part, an inside job. Normally, the Lindberghs spent the workweek in Englewood and stayed at their own home only on the weekends. However, the family had remained at the home near Hopewell until Tuesday because the baby had a cold. The question thus arose: How did the kidnapper know the baby would be at home? And how did he know which window to enter?

Investigators first detained the boyfriend of Betty Gow, the baby's nurse, but soon concluded he was an unlikely suspect. Attention then focused on Violet Sharpe, a 28-year-old English woman who worked as a waitress for Mrs. Morrow at the Englewood estate. All of the staff at the Morrow home had been told that the Lindberghs would be staying in Hopewell because of the baby's cold. Anyone of them could, presumably, have passed that information on to the kidnapper, but it was Violet who gave contradictory testimony and could not explain her whereabouts on the night of the kidnapping.

After receiving what Schwarzkopf described as "contrary and evasive" statements from Violet Sharpe, investigators called the Morrow estate to say they were returning to question the young waitress again. For whatever reason, Violet could not bear the ordeal. She took a can of cyanide-based crystals designed to clean silver, mixed them with water, and drank. By the time the police arrived, Violet was dead. Mrs. Morrow, Anne's mother, and others insisted she had been "frightened to death," but the police interpreted her death as an indication she had been part of the plot, or at least knew more than she had told. Noting that she had become morose after the baby's death, some theorized that she had been part of the conspiracy but had expected the child to be returned safely once the ransom had been paid. But no one had more than speculation to draw on. Contrary to the charges of Mrs. Morrow and the London newspapers—inflamed over the alleged harassment of a British subject—Schwarzkopf denied the police had badgered Violet. Although Violet had fainted once during questioning, Schwarzkopf insisted that she was "always treated gently, never roughly."

Anne and Charles Lindbergh did not believe Violet knew anything about the kidnapping and murder of their son. Lindbergh's explanation apparently was the accurate one. The aviator believed that the anxiety-ridden young woman, who had been having affairs with as many as five men, was shamed over being grilled about her personal life. Violet felt disgraced, feared that she would be fired by Mrs. Morrow, and ultimately deported back to England. "Life is getting so sad I really don't think there is much to live for anymore," she wrote to her sister in the days before the suicide.

Schwarzkopf sought to continue his investigation of the servants, but after Violet's death Anne and her mother put a stop to what they considered harassment of their loyal staff. Stymied, the police could not carry out as full an investigation as they wanted of the servants, including a Morrow family assistant chauffeur, Charles Henry Ellerson, who had driven Betty Gow to Hopewell on the day of the kidnapping. Ellerson had been seen in a New Jersey speakeasy flashing large rolls of cash, but no persuasive evidence materialized linking him to the kidnapping.

The Lindberghs tried to move on with their lives, but Charles remained obsessed with the case. He slept and ate little, losing as much as thirty pounds from his already lanky frame. The investigation continued throughout 1933 and into 1934, but consisted mostly of a series of false leads and hoaxes that left Lindbergh and Schwarzkopf frustrated.

The break in the case came as a result of one of the financial reforms of Franklin Roosevelt's New Deal. In early April 1933, the president signed the Banking Relief Act mandating that all persons possessing gold bullion, gold coins, or certificates valued at more than $100 turn them in to the Federal Reserve. Marked gold certificates, stamped with a distinctive yellow seal, made up two-thirds of the cash paid to "Graveyard John." Over the course of the next year, Lindbergh bills turned up with regularity at Federal Reserve depositories. Investigators closed in. In September 1934, a grocer reported that a man matching Condon's description of the kidnapper had cashed a $10 gold certificate for a 6-cent purchase. By this time the Bureau of Investigation, sure that Graveyard John drove a car, had sent a circular to New York service stations advising attendants to record the license numbers of autos whose drivers paid with the now illegal gold certificates.

Finally, on September 15, 1934, a man driving a blue 1930 Dodge sedan paid for a dollar's worth of gas with a $10 gold certificate that, under the new law, should already have been turned in. The service station attendant recorded the driver's license number, and the New York State Motor Vehicles Bureau provided the name and address of the car's owner: Bruno Richard Hauptmann, 1279 East 222nd Street, the Bronx. Bureau of Investigation officials proceeded to Hauptmann's house and summoned J. Edgar Hoover to New York. He immediately took credit for the arrest of the alleged Lindbergh baby kidnapper.

Hauptmann, a German immigrant and carpenter, was a well-built man with dark blonde hair, a triangular shaped face with a small mouth, and almond-shaped eyes—all of which fit Condon's description. His wallet contained a $20 gold certificate from the Lindbergh ransom. Inside the house Hauptmann had several maps, including one for New Jersey and the Massachusetts coastal waters where the "boad" *Nelly* was supposed to have been moored. The subsequent investigation showed that Hauptmann had quit carpentry shortly after the kidnapping, explaining to his wife Anna that he had invested so well in the stock market that he no longer needed to work. Anna herself had gone on a trip to Germany while Hauptmann had enjoyed a Florida vacation and a Maine hunting trip. He had also bought himself an expensive radio, a hunting rifle, a canoe, and other items.

The most damning evidence, however, lay hidden in the walls of the Hauptmann garage. By the time investigators dismantled the structure, they had found $14,600 of the Lindbergh bank notes as well as a loaded pistol. Hauptmann, who initially denied possession of any of the Lindbergh money, now explained that he had merely been given charge of the money for safekeeping by a friend of his, Isidor Fisch, who had returned to Germany and died. Hauptmann could not explain why he had scrawled Condon's address and telephone number on his bedroom-closet wall. He continued to protest his innocence, but at a police lineup Condon identified Hauptmann as Graveyard John, although the eccentric doctor refused to make a positive declaration while the press hovered in the vicinity. He later testified that he knew from the moment he saw him that Hauptmann was John.

Relieved by the news of John's capture, Lindbergh arranged to have a look at the alleged kidnapper while he underwent questioning. Disguising himself in a hat and dark glasses, Lindbergh sat in on an interview with detectives, who compelled Hauptmann to say the words, "Hey, Doctor, over here," which Lindbergh had heard when he had accompanied Condon with the ransom money. Lindbergh later described Hauptmann as "a magnificent-looking man, splendidly built, but with the eyes of a wild boar—mean, shifty, small and cruel."

In the subsequent murder trial in Flemington, New Jersey, both Lindbergh and Dr. Condon positively identified Hauptmann as Graveyard John. Prosecution witnesses also placed Hauptmann on the roads near Hopewell in the days leading up to the kidnapping, and some even remembered seeing a folded-up ladder in his vehicle. Hauptmann had repainted the vehicle from green to blue shortly after the kidnapping. A Bronx cabdriver testified that Hauptmann hired him to take one of the sealed ransom notes to Condon's house.

Hauptmann's background also bolstered the prosecution's case, directed by New Jersey Attorney General David Wilentz. From Kamenz, Saxony, Hauptmann had served in the Great War as a machine gunner, which made him something of an elite warrior responsible for myriad kills. Two of his brothers died in the war. He displayed a special interest in wartime aviators, especially Baron Manfred Albrecht von Richthofen, Germany's top ace, for whom Hauptmann would name his son. Only nineteen when the war ended, Hauptmann, like many Germans, faced a grim existence marked by high unemployment and critical shortages of food. Together with another war veteran, he turned to crime.

In one incident in Germany, which the prosecution in the Lindbergh case naturally called to attention, Hauptmann used a ladder to gain entry to a second-story window to steal 300 marks and a silver watch. On another occasion Hauptmann robbed women pushing strollers full of food, waving a gun and threatening to shoot. Apprehended, he spent four years in jail before being paroled. Accused of theft soon thereafter and lodged in a local jail, Hauptmann escaped, leaving a taunting note for the police, and attempted to stow away on ships bound for New York. Twice he failed, once having to jump overboard and swim to shore to avoid arrest in a German port. On the third try Hauptmann succeeded and walked ashore in New York in 1923 carrying a stolen landing card. Hauptmann's record thus revealed a criminal past marked by boldness, determination, and a modus operandi similar to that used in the Lindbergh case.

Although the evidence was, in Lindbergh's judgment, "overwhelming," the defense, led by noted criminal attorney Edward Reilly, tried to shift suspicion to other individuals, including Condon and the servants. (At one point the erratic Reilly insisted that the butler had done it.) More than 600 people jammed into the stuffy courtroom in Flemington, including visitors from Europe. Visitors clogged the roads into the tiny New Jersey town. Outside, hundreds of people milled about, families ate picnic lunches, and vendors hawked souvenirs, including small wooden ladders and "genuine" locks of the dead baby's hair.

The trial, of course, was a wrenching ordeal for the Lindberghs. Anne appeared only twice: on the first day of the proceedings and later to testify about the scene at home on the night of the kidnapping. Lindbergh himself attended every day, filing through the crowds of reporters and photographers, sometimes armed with a pistol that he now carried for protection. He appeared grim but focused on the proceedings, ignoring the press and the crush of people around him.

In addition to the positive identifications by Condon, Lindbergh, and those who had seen Hauptmann around Hopewell, seven handwriting experts testified that it was obvious that the same person wrote all fourteen ransom notes. Noting that the same spelling errors and transposition of letters as in "singnature" appeared in several of the notes, one graphologist declared that the conclusion that one man had written all of them was "irresistible, unanswerable, and overwhelming." Prosecutor Wilentz found a written example of Hauptmann writing "boad" on a document separate from the ransom notes. The prosecutor followed up that evidence by prompting Hauptmann to make similar misspellings and transposition of letters on the witness stand.

The prosecution also destroyed Hauptmann's claim to gains in stock investments. In fact, the carpenter had actually lost $9,132.29. Wilentz showed that the three-fourth-inch chisel, found in the Lindbergh yard, fit into an empty space in Hauptmann's tool chest. Finally, the chief wood expert for the U.S. Forest Service, Arthur Koehler, testified that one of the ladder's rails matched the wood in the floor of Hauptmann's attic.

Defense witnesses took the stand in Hauptmann's behalf, but none could swear that he had been anywhere else on the evening of March 1. Near the end of his six-hour cross-examination of the defendant, Wilentz tried but failed to induce Hauptmann to confess. Tension over the sharp exchange of questions and answers filled the courtroom, with both Wilentz and Hauptmann raising their voices. "You wouldn't tell (confess) if they murdered you, would you?" Wilentz finally shouted. In a flash Hauptmann shot back, "No!"

Wilentz had beautifully marshaled the evidence, but marred his performance with a xenophobic summation in which he asked, "What type of man would murder the child of Charles and Anne Lindbergh? He wouldn't be an American." In his instructions to the jury, the presiding judge, Thomas Trenchard, spoke favorably of the prosecution's case while casting doubt on the testimony of defense witnesses. While the jury deliberated, demonstrators outside the courthouse chanted, "Kill Hauptmann! Kill Hauptmann!" Lindbergh himself described the throng as a "lynching crowd."

After more than eleven hours of deliberations, the jury returned with a verdict of guilty on February 13, 1935, ending the six-week Hauptmann trial. Most of the jury's discussion had concerned not guilt, on which they concurred, but the sentencing. By making no specific recommendation for life imprisonment, the conviction for first-degree murder meant that Hauptmann would face the electric chair.

When news of the verdict came over the radio at the Morrow family home, a shaken Anne snapped, "Charles, turn that off." Lindbergh then "very quietly, very simply," as family friend Harold Nicolson recalled, "went through the case point by point." Lindbergh assured his family that "There is no doubt at all that Hauptmann did the thing." The aviator explained that he had dreaded the possibility "that they would get hold of someone as a victim about whom I wasn't sure. I am sure about this—quite sure." As Nicolson recalled, Lindbergh's recapitulation of the facts of the case "seemed to relieve all of them."

Despite the overwhelming evidence against Hauptmann, many sympathized with the handsome German immigrant, seeing him as a victim of World War I, in which—while still a teenager—he had been compelled to serve. Beyond question his trial had been conducted in a circus atmosphere, with 70,000 to 100,000 people, including celebrities, descending on the tiny New Jersey town. The trial featured tears and outbursts from the gallery, grandstanding by the attorneys, and a sea of writers and photographers sometimes literally fighting their way into the courtroom. (In the wake of the Hauptmann trial states began to proscribe the use of cameras during courtroom proceedings.) The acerbic journalist H. L. Mencken called it "the most important event since the Resurrection."

Most Americans applauded the verdict, although the German-American community, especially in New York, expressed outrage. German Americans raised money for the appeal process, cheered Anna Hauptmann when she appeared at rallies in her husband's behalf, and booed loudly when they heard the name Lindbergh. It was true, as German Americans charged, that the circus atmosphere cried for vengeance, and Hauptmann's foreign birth and imperfect grasp of English had worked against him in the trial. But unlike the case of Sacco and Vanzetti in 1927, the evidence of Hauptmann's guilt, though much of it circumstantial, was compelling.

As with any famous—indeed infamous—crime, controversy was, and remains, inevitable. Hauptmann's widow insisted for decades on her husband's innocence. Authors weighed in with books such as Anthony Scaduto's *Scapegoat* (1976), which attempted to exonerate Hauptmann despite the evidence against him. Wild theories found their way into print. One holds that Anne's older sister Elisabeth, insanely jealous over Charles's selection of Anne instead of her, orchestrated the kidnap and murder of the Lindbergh baby. Another theory asserts that Lindbergh killed his own child accidentally, while attempting a practical joke. Such accounts, however baseless, are inevitable in an age of tabloid journalism, but the evidence against Hauptmann cannot be ignored.

Hauptmann went to his death without confessing to the crime. Indeed, he insisted on his innocence to the end, claiming that he was a sacrificial lamb for the public's desire for vengeance. Despite the intervention of New Jersey governor Harold Hoffman, who suggested that Hauptmann was innocent and met secretly with the condemned man in his cell, time ran out on the Kamenz carpenter. After several stays of execution, Hoffman backed out of the case and the U.S. Supreme Court rejected Hauptmann's final appeal. As scores of witnesses looked on, Hauptmann, apologizing to no one, wearing his prison clothes and with his head shaved, took his place in the electric chair at the New Jersey State Penitentiary. At a little past 9 on Friday night, April 3, 1936, he was put to death for the murder of Charles Augustus Lindbergh, Jr.

5

Expatriate

Even before the murder of their son and the Hauptmann trial, the Lindberghs found it difficult to attain any degree of privacy. Those sensational events made it almost impossible. The only sure way of avoiding the press and public was to escape through the air. Throughout the 1930s Lindbergh, with Anne as his copilot, welcomed the opportunity to continue his pioneering work in aviation while exploring the far reaches of the globe.

Within months of their wedding in 1929, Anne had become a skilled pilot under Charles's tutelage. As the Lindberghs criss-crossed the continent and ventured abroad, they established themselves, in the words of a *Vanity Fair* article, as America's "first romancers of the air." Anne showed herself to be a first-rate pilot, navigator, and radio operator. There was little that she, like her intrepid husband, would not try. When Lindbergh, becoming increasingly fascinated by motorless flight, obtained his license as a glider pilot, becoming only the seventh American to do so, Anne was right behind him. She became the first American woman to obtain a license as a glider pilot—and did so while six months pregnant.

Anne was the most famous flying wife and mother in the country, as well as the most gifted writer among women aviators. She was one of scores of women, led by the legendary

Amelia Earhart, who found the independence in flight that patriarchal American society frequently denied women on the ground. By the early thirties Earhart led a generation of prominent women flyers, including Anne Morrow Lindbergh. By joining her husband on a series of daring flights, which she then chronicled in her evocative prose, Anne advanced the role of women in aviation history.

The flying Lindberghs made a series of national and overseas flights, often setting new speed records. As he had done in preparation for his New York to Paris flight, Lindbergh went to California to supervise the building of a new aircraft, a Lockheed monoplane that the Lindberghs named *Sirius,* the brightest star in the sky. Although the plane was heavy, it could fly at 185 miles per hour with a range of over 2,000 miles. On April 20, 1930, the Lindberghs boarded *Sirius,* newly painted in black with orange trim, and flew to New York in fourteen hours and forty-five minutes. Flying at high altitude, which Lindbergh believed was "safest and fastest" because it allowed pilots to go above storms, the couple shattered the existing record of transcontinental flight by three hours. However, Anne—almost seven months pregnant—became ill and had to be carried from the plane after arrival in New York. In the ensuing press coverage, some reporters emphasized her illness more than the new speed record.

The Lindberghs did not spend all their airtime on commercial aviation. While Charles had taught Anne to fly and navigate, she had much to teach him as well. Drawing on the Morrow family's long-held interest in archaeology and ancient cultures, Anne discussed these matters with her husband, who responded with enthusiasm. The Lindberghs frequently made archaeological excursions by air into remote areas of the American Southwest and Central America. Charles, who had become enamored with aerial photography, snapped pictures of little-known Mayan ruins in Guatemala while Anne expertly tilted their aircraft to set up the shots. The couple's efforts, publicized nationally, called attention to the value of using aircraft reconnaissance to aid exploration of archaeological sites. The Lindberghs reveled in these experiences, sometimes setting down their plane to march off on grueling expeditions exploring the remains of ancient cultures. Anne walked for miles in the desert, scaled cliffs with her husband, camped out in the wild, and found little about which to complain.

Their boldest adventure was a 1931 flight from New York to China, a mission designed to lay the groundwork for commercial air travel to East Asia. Instead of flying west, the Lindberghs would go north by way of the Great Circle route. Instead of flying west, they would fly north. Lindbergh had always found Arctic routes "tantalizing" because they reduced flying time and avoided long stretches over ocean waters. In 1930 he began to chart a course north from New York through Canada; across the frozen lakes of the Northwest Territories to Alaska; south to the Kamchatka Peninsula of the USSR; down the Kurile Islands to Tokyo; then on to the interior of China.

By late July 1931, Lindbergh had completed his usual painstaking preparations. Every item, from their emergency rubber raft to the food they would eat, had been carefully selected and weighed. He equipped *Sirius* with pontoons, since few landing facilities existed along the route. The burdens of a heavy load would be compounded by having to take off from water, but the specially ordered 575-horsepower Cyclone engine made by the Wright Aeronautical Corporation was up to the task. Anne, leaving Charles, Jr., in the care of nannies, would serve as radio operator.

As Anne recounted in her critically acclaimed book, *North to the Orient* (1935), the Lindberghs endured so many perilous moments on the Great Circle flight that she nicknamed her husband "Charles the Invincible." The couple plowed through white-out blizzards, repeatedly lost radio contact, and three times survived harrowing forced landings. Any one of the three might have resulted in disaster for a less skilled pilot than Lindbergh, but before it was over he had flown more than 10,000 miles with no irreparable damage to his plane.

The most serious threat came on the ground in China, near the end of the trip, when the Lindberghs offered to assist in flood relief flights. The Yangtze River, sweeping over its banks, had inundated several villages, destroyed roads and crops, leaving many desperate and starving. One one occasion, leaving Anne behind, Lindbergh flew with two physicians to Xinghua in Jiangsu Province. As the doctors handed out medicines in the harbor, sampans carrying starving villagers converged on *Sirius,* threatening to damage the plane's pontoons. When one villager moved to board the plane, Lindbergh unholstered a pistol and fired a warning shot. The Chinese fell back long enough for him to maneuver the plane free of the sampans and take off.

The Great Circle flight ended ignominiously, through no fault of the Lindberghs, when the plane slipped from its mechanicial moorings while being lowered into the water at Hankow. Both Charles and Anne had to leap from *Sirius* and swim to shore. Soon after, they received more shocking news: a death in the family. Anne's father, Dwight Morrow, by then a New Jersey senator, died of a stroke on October 5, 1931, at age fifty-eight, prompting the Lindberghs to return home.

The Asian flight marked another in the series of aviation milestones for Lindbergh. Charles and Anne had enjoyed a fascinating adventure while contributing significantly to existing knowledge of arctic flight. Years later, after World War II, Northwest Orient Airlines followed the Lindberghs' pioneering path in charting its New York-to-Tokyo commercial service. After their return from China, the Lindberghs rested at the Morrow estate and spent a few months with Charles, Jr.

Following the kidnapping in March and the discovery of the child's body in May, the investigation proceeded haltingly, prompting the Lindberghs to deal with their grief by escaping once again to the air. After the birth of their second son, Jon, in August 1932, Charles and Anne set off on a trip surveying northern routes to Europe. Lindbergh added an even larger, 710-horsepower engine and new navigation and radio equipment to the giant seaplane, which they now renamed *Tingmissartog,* an Inuit name meaning "one who flies like a large bird."

Departing in July 1933, the Lindberghs flew up the North American coast over Labrador and across to Greenland, Iceland, and the Shetland Islands. While flying the northern leg of the journey, Lindbergh, who was developing a compelling interest in biology, made the first successful spore and bacteria survey of the air over the North Atlantic. The aviator had invented the "sky hook," a device that allowed him to collect airborne spores and bacteria on a slide, which could then be taken to labs for analysis. After his return, scientists credited Lindbergh with furthering knowledge about the diffusion of microscopic organisms.

After crossing the Atlantic, the Lindberghs took a leisurely tour of Europe from Scandinavia to Moscow. On their way back from Russia, Charles and Anne toured Britain, France, Holland, Spain, and Switzerland before starting back across the Atlantic through the Azores. The aviators veered south and west again, touring the Canary Islands and Cape Verde before landing on the Gambia River in West Africa. There they received a scare as the heavy plane's pontoons sank deeply in the water, making takeoff from the river impossible. Lindbergh concluded he had no choice but to strip down the plane, throwing all but essential items overboard. He even used shears to tear off a reserve fuel tank before successfully lifting the plane out of the water after a long run in semi-darkness. From the African coast the couple flew across south Atlantic equatorial waters on a direct flight to Natal, Brazil. They proceeded through the Amazon River valley before veering north to Trinidad, then once again up the Antilles to Miami, and home.

The Atlantic survey flight, lasting almost half a year, had been one of Lindbergh's most successful tours. It laid the groundwork for Pan American's trans-Atlantic service across Bermuda and the Azores, which Lindbergh had identified as the best route. The Lindberghs recorded a wealth of information that benefited the cause of commercial aviation. The Atlantic trip offered sharp contrasts between developed European societies and tiny tropical villages whose residents had never seen nor even heard of an airplane. Once again Anne furthered her literary career with a beautifully written account titled *Listen! The Wind* (1938), to which Charles added a foreword.

As always during a long Lindbergh flight, at various points during the journey the couple was reported missing. Relieved by their safe return, much of the public concurred with editorials pleading with them to remain safely on the ground. Eager to spend time with their second son, the Lindberghs lived in seclusion at the Morrow estate, Next Day Hill. Having left their new home near Hopewell after the kidnapping, never to return, they decided to donate the house and property to the state of New Jersey. To that end they created a nonprofit corporation called High Fields and offered the home "to provide for the welfare of children . . . without discrimination in regard to race or creed." The Lindbergh house remains a home for New Jersey youth.

When not engaged with the Hauptmann trial or conducting aerial surveys, Lindbergh spent much of his time in the 1930s indulging a new obsession: biology. Few had taken Lindbergh seriously when he declared that he wanted to be a scientist rather than a mere adventurer, but he soon proved his critics wrong. During his youth on the Minnesota farm, Lindbergh had developed an interest in biology through his observations of the varying habits and behavior of different animals. On one occasion, when Lindbergh discovered a dead horse on the farm, he analyzed the open carcass with fascination.

Contemplation of life and death came naturally to Lindbergh. As an aviation pioneer, he confronted the possibility of death virtually every time he flew. During his flight to Paris, he could only stay awake by reminding himself that the alternative was death. The murder of his child, whose corpse he had carefully examined, and the death of Anne's sister, Elisabeth, after an emergency appendectomy in 1934, spurred Lindbergh on to scientific research. His tremendous accomplishments in aviation inspired such confidence that Lindbergh set out to explore life and death in an attempt to conquer new frontiers in medical research.

Before her death, Anne's sister Elisabeth developed a lesion on her heart. When Lindbergh conferred with her doctors in 1930, he asked why it would not be possible to create a mechanical heart that might keep the body functioning while surgery was performed on the organ. None of the physicians with whom he spoke could explain to Lindbergh why such a procedure would not be possible. Insistent as always, Lindbergh kept probing until a physician referred him to Dr. Alexis Carrel at New York's Rockefeller Institute for Medical Research.

Lindbergh arranged a meeting with Carrel, head of experimental surgery and winner of the 1912 Nobel Prize. Carrel told the aviator that he had been trying for two decades to devise an apparatus that would preserve isolated organs without infection. Required to accomplish this aim was development of a "perfusion pump," a device that would keep organs functional even after their removal from the body. This notion fascinated Lindbergh, who examined the perfusion apparatuses that had been developed up to that time and found them crude. Carrel offered Lindbergh use of his New York laboratory if he wanted to make the effort to develop a successful perfusion pump.

Delighted by the opportunity to work with Carrel, Lindbergh accepted at once. "By contributing my understanding of mechanical design," Lindbergh recalled in his autobiography, "I could work side by side with a man who was a philosopher, a mystic, and one of the greatest experimental surgeons in the world." A long friendship between two men, both highly successful nonconformists, had begun. Years later both said they knew at their first meeting that they would forge a close relationship. They were very different men—one in his late fifties, a short and stocky Frenchman, balding, wearing pince-nez, and a man of science; the other young, tall, lean, and handsome, an American adventurer. Despite the differences, Carrel and Lindbergh shared an instantaneous rapport. They collaborated for more than a decade.

Working with Carrel brought to mind experiences with another older man of research whom Lindbergh had deeply respected—his Grandfather Land. Lindbergh had relished the many hours he had passed as a youth watching his grandfather work in his Detroit dental laboratory. The mature Lindbergh could now take an active role himself. For some five years the aviator spent much of his time in Carrel's laboratory, conversing, studying cells, and regularly donning a black, hooded operating gown to witness Carrel's surgical research. While watching Carrel operate, Lindbergh gushed in his autobiography, "I felt I had reached a frontier where the mystical and the scientific meet, where I would see across the indistinct border separating life from death."

As he drove from New Jersey to the New York laboratory, Lindbergh contemplated nothing less than unlocking the secrets of life. His own experience demonstrated that humanity was well on the way to conquering air and space. He now envisioned "the ability of science to solve the origins of existence." Lindbergh worked compulsively, often from morning to midnight, and frequently spent nights at the lab. "If I could design a better perfusion pump," Lindbergh thought, "I could keep those organs alive long after the body they supported had entered the state called 'death.'" Infection from bacteria and poisoning from the wastes of the living tissue were the main obstacles.

After five years of meticulous research and experimentation, Lindbergh developed a perfusion pump that preserved a chicken's carotid artery for a month. The device designed by Lindbergh was quite sophisticated and remained the state of the art for decades. In April 1935 Carrel and Lindbergh successfully cultivated in vitro the thyroid gland of a cat. For the first time, they had succeeded in freeing organs from infection, allowing them to be preserved at about the same pressures as in real-life conditions.

Lindbergh had managed to keep his relationship with Dr. Carrel secret for almost five years, but *Time* magazine lauded the two researchers in a 1935 cover story. Medical journals took note of their research. In 1937 Lindbergh collaborated with Carrel on a book, *The Culture of Organs* (1938). The two wrote alternate chapters, with Lindbergh focusing on the design, construction, and function of the perfusion pump, while Carrel put their research into a scientific context. By the late thirties Lindbergh's accomplishments in medical research, added to his unparalleled achievements in aviation, marked the height of his prestige.

Although Lindbergh and Carrel collaborated successfully in their scientific investigations, their relationship may not have been entirely positive. Both men were talented iconoclasts who tended to reinforce the prejudices and noncomformist streaks that each strongly held. Lindbergh had been drawn to Carrel in part because of his willingness to employ radical methodologies, and take an almost mystical approach to his work, rather than adhering to traditional scientific methods. When extended to the realm of social philosophy, Carrel's eccentric views disturbed many. In a book titled *Man, the Unknown* (1935) Carrel asserted that human society should be shepherded by a minority of enlightened elites who would put what he called realism ahead of sentimentalism. Violent criminals and the mentally ill would be put to death in state institutions. Such philosophic musings were not novel, but Carrel's advocacy of them, coinciding with the rise of European fascism, proved unsettling to many. To a considerable extent, Lindbergh shared Carrel's doubts about democratic society.

Lindbergh remained friends with Carrel until the French scientist's death in 1944, but the two drifted apart after publication of their book as Lindbergh became more interested in world affairs than in scientific research. The collaboration with Carrel showed the extent to which Lindbergh admired men who, like himself, bucked convention, anticipated the future, and were considered mavericks.

Another figure who fit this description was an obscure physics professor at Clark University, Robert H. Goddard. Charles Lindbergh, more than anyone else, recognized the significance of Goddard's work and thus helped inspire revolutionary developments in rocketry. Ever since he had taken up gliding, Lindbergh had learned everything he could about motorless flight. "I realized the limits of the propeller, and this led me into the field of rockets and jet propulsion," he later explained.

Informed in 1929 that Goddard, in the course of his experiments, had fired a liquid-fueled rocket 100 feet in the air, Lindbergh promptly journeyed to Worcester, Massachusetts, to meet with him. Impressed, Lindbergh set up meetings with Daniel Guggenheim, the wealthy father of his close friend Harry Guggenheim, to arrange financial support for Goddard's research. Lindbergh also approached the U.S. military establishment, but unlike Lindbergh the men there failed to see the awesome potential of rocketry. While the military declined to support Goddard's research, Daniel Guggenheim, on the basis of Lindbergh's recommendation, contributed over the next decade some $148,000 through various foundations.

Lindbergh, who had joined Harry Guggenheim, Orville Wright, and others as a member of the National Advisory Committee for Aeronautics, closely monitored tests carried out by Goddard at new proving grounds near Roswell, New Mexico. By the late thirties Lindbergh had reason to suspect the advance of German rocketry, adding urgency to Goddard's experiments. Goddard made steady progress, culminating in 1941 when he launched a rocket 9,000 feet into the air. Throughout this period Lindbergh had kept quiet his activity in Goddard's behalf. Thus, his efforts did not become known until the 1963 publication of a biography on Goddard. By that time the father of modern rocketry had more than 200 patents to his credit. Lindbergh admired Goddard, who like himself marked great achievements after others had insisted they could not be accomplished. Never before, Lindbergh declared, had he been so impressed by "one man's effort and almost superhuman vision in a field of science so fantastic in his day that anyone venturing much confidence in its future was considered unscientific."

While Lindbergh respected and supported scientists, visionaries, and individualists, he had little respect for politicians. Lindbergh voted Republican and had personal relationships with both presidents Coolidge and Hoover. The aviation hero endorsed the latter publicly in both 1928 and 1932. Now a man of wealth and prestige, Lindbergh, unlike his father, spent little time concerning himself over the plight of less fortunate Americans. He was not a supporter of President Franklin D. Roosevelt and the New Deal, which beginning in 1933 attempted, with only limited success, to ameliorate the misery of the Great Depression.

Although himself wealthy, Roosevelt was not above denouncing "economic royalists," whom much of the public blamed for the devastating economic collapse. By the time the new president took office, a congressional investigation with Ferdinand Pecora as counsel had revealed myriad instances of corrupt business practices that contributed to both the stock market crash and the collapse of the nation's banking system. Charges of corruption and fraud on the part of great corporations and speculators resonated with a public angry over the depressed economy.

The Pecora investigation had little impact on Lindbergh, but another probe, directed by Alabama senator Hugo Black, led to the first of several sharp confrontations between the aviation hero and President Roosevelt. Senator Black's committee uncovered corruption in federal air mail contracts and charged that big business collusion had driven out smaller competitors. Roosevelt's Postmaster General, James A. Farley, cited TWA—"the Lindbergh Line"—as one of the major offenders. To the accompaniment of widespread publicity, investigators charged that the major airlines, benefiting from lack of competitive bidding under the Hoover administration, had overcharged the government. TWA's charges were said to exceed the bids of smaller airline companies by more than $5 million. Senator Black urged Roosevelt to cancel federal air mail contracts. After receiving clearance from his attorney general, and assurance from the chief of the Army Air Corps that its pilots could assume the burden of flying air mail, Roosevelt took Black's advice.

Stunned by the president's executive order of February 9, 1934, Lindbergh interpreted FDR's action as a personal attack, since his name was associated with TWA and had been mentioned in the course of the Black committee probe. "Your action of yesterday affects fundamentally the industry to which I have devoted the last twelve years of my life," Lindbergh told the president in a sharply worded telegram in February 1934. He charged that FDR's action "condemns the largest portion of our commercial aviation without a just trial." Lindbergh insisted that the federal air mail program had furthered the general progress of American aviation, which the president's executive order now threatened to "greatly damage."

Roosevelt had not anticipated a stinging rebuke from the one man in America who matched his own popularity. The president also resented that Lindbergh, somewhat hypocritically given his well-known contempt for the press, had provided copies of his telegram to reporters. Most newspapers and radio commentators echoed Lindbergh's criticisms. FDR, who had won over the American people through his soothing fireside chats, had suffered one of the first setbacks of his presidency at the hands of Charles Lindbergh. He would neither forget nor forgive the aviation hero.

Both Roosevelt and Lindbergh had some justification for their positions. Lindbergh never came to grips with the Black committee's findings of overcharging and corruption. It was almost as if the aviator considered them irrelevant. By decrying the absence of a "fair trial," Lindbergh, as one senator pointed out to him, displayed ignorance of the difference between criminal and civil procedure in American jurisprudence. Former general Billy Mitchell condemned the commercial carriers as "profiteers" who exploited federal subsidies. He claimed that Lindbergh, by defending them, "has disclosed himself as the 'front man' for the Air Trust" and a man who cared only about profits.

As a major stockholder in commercial airlines, Lindbergh indeed concerned himself with profits, but pilot safety mattered even more. It soon became clear that he had been correct in his insistence that the Army Air Corps was not equipped to fly the nation's mails. The army pilots, as Lindbergh well knew, had not been as well prepared to perform their tasks as commercial pilots. Within their first week of operations, complicated by bad weather, five army pilots had been killed; six critically injured; and eight aircraft had been destroyed. By the beginning of April, twelve army pilots had been killed and forty-six forced landings of air mail planes had occurred. Another American aviation hero, World War I ace Eddie Rickenbacker, who had joined Eastern Airlines, called Roosevelt's action "legalized murder." Aviation was still a perilous business and commercial planes also went down periodically, to be sure. Eight persons had died, for example, not long before in a United Airlines crash in Utah. Still, as Lindbergh and Rickenbacker argued, army pilots had not received proper training and their planes lacked the sophisticated radio equipment standard on commercial airlines.

In testimony at highly publicized congressional hearings in March, Lindbergh advocated returning federal mail to private carriers. Under pressure from the aviation hero, the press, and much of the public following the series of army air disasters, Roosevelt retracted his executive order. However, by the end of 1934 the federal airline subsidy had been slashed from $19.4 million in 1933 to $8 million. Lindbergh and Roosevelt had fought to a draw, but conflict between the two would resume on the eve of U.S. involvement in World War II.

The air mail controversy, together with the Hauptmann trial, made 1934 onerous for the Lindberghs. They continued to suffer from intrusions on their privacy. The aviator was no longer surprised to read verbatim in the next day's newspaper what he had said in the course of table conversation at a private dinner—a result of press payments to other guests in exchange for their stories. Lindbergh had no choice but to endure such intrusions, but he and Anne were determined to protect their second son at all costs.

With the birth of Jon in August 1932, Lindbergh issued a statement explaining that while the family wished to continue living in New Jersey, it would be "impossible for us to subject the life of our second son to the publicity which we feel was in large measure responsible for the death of our first." The aviator appealed to the press "to permit our children to lead the lives of normal Americans." Partly in response to periodic threats by unknown persons to kidnap his second son, Lindbergh hired bodyguards and bought a menacing German shepherd named Thor.

Even these steps failed to deter journalists. On one occasion, while three-year-old Jon cavorted with other children on his Englewood nursery school playground, a truck with a large canvas-covered bed parked alongside. The teachers feared the truck might contain kidnappers, but those inside were actually press photographers snapping pictures of the child through slits in the canvas. More frightening still, soon thereafter a vehicle forced onto the shoulder of the road the automobile being driven by Jon's nurse, who was taking him home from school. As the nurse, fearing kidnappers, screamed, a stream of photographers burst from the other car, crammed their cameras into the windows, and took pictures of the sobbing child.

These events coincided with New Jersey Governor Harold Hoffman's reckless intrusion in the Hauptmann case. The governor publicly gave credence to some of the more ludicrous kidnap-conspiracy theories, prompting the Trenton *Times* and a group of Princeton academics, including the university president, to call for his impeachment. His actions threatened to drag out the Hauptmann case even after the conviction had been handed down. All of these events, and a steady stream of threats and demands of ransom to guarantee Jon's safe treatment, prompted Lindbergh to order passports for the family. As he recalled years later, "I decided to take my family abroad until conditions in my own country changed enough to let me establish a reasonably safe and happy home life for them."

Lindbergh thus became the country's most prominent expatriate. Columnist Walter Lippmann wrote that the Lindberghs were "refugees from the tyranny of yellow journalism" and had been denied their "inalienable right to privacy." In December 1935, having heard that they could escape public intrusions in England, the Lindberghs packed their belongings and left New York. Settling in the garden country of Kent, on an estate called "Long Barn," the family finally got the peace they craved. Jon had room to play and the English villagers, as advertised, respected their privacy. Charles and Anne traveled frequently to London and dined with the royal family, some of whom Lindbergh had met after his historic Paris flight. However, they could always return home to seclusion.

The Lindberghs developed a few friends, including historian Harold Nicholson and his wife, Vita Sackville-West, owners of Long Barn. For more than three years, Charles and Anne corresponded with American friends and associates, returning to the States only for brief periods, and secretly if possible. Lindbergh sometimes missed his work with Carrel at the Rockefeller Institute, but recalled that "Most of all I missed the opportunity of working closely with Robert Goddard in developing rockets that I felt might someday carry man out into space."

The Lindberghs, peripatetic as always, traveled all over Europe and to India, even though Anne was in the latter stages of pregnancy. After their return in May 1937 she bore her third son, Land Morrow Lindbergh. In the summer of 1938 Lindbergh, on a recommendation from Dr. Carrel, purchased the storm-washed island of Illiec off the northern coast of Brittany. There they lived for weeks with no running water or electric lights, but with the privacy they treasured. Carrel, who owned a home on a nearby island, observed that the Lindberghs required solitude as part of the healing process from the kidnapping, trial, and attendant publicity. Because of their "great misfortune," he explained, Lindbergh himself had become "hypersensitive and wants only quiet and to be forgotten. . . . He has suffered enough."

While at Long Barn and Illiec, Anne concentrated on her writing while Lindbergh spent much of his time contrasting the various European cultures observed during his frequent travels. Lindbergh blamed much of his family's troubles on American society and compared his native country with the European nations he visited. He appreciated the civility shown by the British, but concluded that England's glory days had passed and that a certain complacency had set in. The Lindberghs enjoyed life in France (from Illiec one could walk to the mainland during low tide). They also spent time in Paris and eventually lived in an apartment there. Lindbergh found France less constrained by tradition than Britain, but a more contentious society, which he attributed to a history marked by excesses such as the French Revolution and the subsequent Napoleonic era.

The most dynamic country in Europe at the time, however, and the one that impressed Lindbergh most, was Nazi Germany. Like many Europeans and Americans at the time, Lindbergh respected certain aspects of German culture and failed to anticipate the fanaticism of the Nazi leader, Adolf Hitler. At the time, Lindbergh recalled, "I was stirred by the spirit in Germany as I had been deadened by the lack of it in England and disturbed by its volatile individuality in France." Like many Westerners, Lindbergh interpreted Germany's new aggressiveness as a natural response to its humiliation in the 1919 Versailles Treaty, whose terms had saddled Germany with a $33 billion reparations bill and responsibility for World War I. Although anti-Semitism was part of Nazi ideology, it seems to have concerned Lindbergh little at the time.

Lindbergh's mounting fascination with Germany stemmed from an invitation he received in 1936 from Major Truman Smith, the U.S. military attaché at the American Embassy in Berlin. That same year Germany had remilitarized the Rhineland, in violation of the Versailles Treaty, and had launched a massive rearmament program. Alarmed by renascent German militarism, which England and France failed to counter, Smith summoned Lindbergh in hopes that the aviator could obtain a reliable estimate of the status of German air power.

Smith knew that Hermann Goering, head of the Luftwaffe, German air force, admired Lindbergh and might be willing to provide more information to the aviation hero than to anyone else. "From a purely American point of view," Smith wrote Lindbergh in May 1936, "I consider that your visit here would be of high patriotic benefit. I am certain that they will go out of their way to show you even more than they will show us." Officially, Lindbergh would be the guest of Lufthansa, the German commercial airline. Nazi officials promised to keep the press clear of his path. With that pledge, the flyer accepted the invitation. He and Anne arrived in Berlin at the end of July, in time to attend opening ceremonies at the 1936 Olympic Games. Many Americans resented their appearance in Berlin even though there was no U.S. boycott of the games. The image of Lindbergh, grim-faced as he departed his native country, now reappeared in press photographs that showed him flashing his broad smile in the company of Nazi leaders.

Lindbergh's nine-day tour of Germany proved a turning point in his life. Just as Truman Smith had expected, the Nazi leaders took the aviation hero on tours of aircraft factories, allowed him to examine and fly warplanes that other Americans would never have been allowed to see. German officials made no attempt to hide their desire to build the world's most powerful air force. The red carpet rolled out for Lindbergh reflected both the Nazi leaders' admiration for him and their desire to impress the United States, through Lindbergh. The Nazis meant to expand German power in Eastern Europe and hoped that demonstrations of their stength would discourage Western interference with those plans. The strategy worked with Lindbergh. Impressed with Nazi air power and efficiency, he concluded that "Germany was preparing for war on a major scale with the most modern equipment."

Viewing firsthand the destructive potential of modern air power proved to be a shattering experience for Lindbergh. Previously, all of his efforts had been directed toward adventure and commercial flying, but his focus now shifted to military aviation. As the threat of war emerged in Europe, Lindbergh "began to think about the vulnerability of men to aircraft carrying high-explosive bombs." He had devoted his life to promoting science and technology as forces of human progress, but now realized that aviation could heap unprecedented destruction on millions of people. His dreams of the shining triumph of aviation had given way to despair.

Lindbergh's first tour of Nazi Germany made a profound impression on him. Although he would soon oppose efforts to impede Germany's eastward expansion, Lindbergh condemned Nazi plans for aggressive war. Called on to make a toast at an Air Ministry luncheon on the third day of his tour, the aviation hero raised his glass and said, "Here's to the bombers, may they get slower. And here's to pursuit planes, may they grow swifter!" In another talk Lindbergh rebuked his hosts for their buildup of air power, warning that advances in aviation threatened to "destroy the very things we wish to protect."

Despite his concern about Nazi militarism, Lindbergh had been impressed with what he saw during his German tour. He spent most of his time with scientists and Luft-waffe officers. As always, he paid little attention to politics and, according to American reporters in Berlin, displayed indifference to Nazi repression. In contrast to what he perceived as the weary British, the fractious French, and an America gone wrong, the Germans appeared united and moving ahead at a swift pace. The compulsive energy of the Nazi regime mirrored Lindbergh's own personality.

By January 1937 Lindbergh concluded that Germany was "in many ways the most interesting nation in the world today." He respected Germany's spirit, order, and technical achievement. He found in the Third Reich a "sense of decency and value which in many ways is far ahead of our own." Although he had not met Hitler, Lindbergh judged him "a great man" who "has done much for the German people." True, Hitler was "a fanatic," but Lindbergh thought some degree of fanaticism inevitable as a result of Germany's treatment after World War I. "When conditions become as chaotic as they were in Germany after the war," he observed, "one must expect fanaticism to result, and hope that moderation comes later."

While Lindbergh was not a fascist, he admired aspects of German and, to a lesser extent, Italian political culture in the 1930s. With the democracies in decline, as Lindbergh saw it, the future would be reduced to a contest between communism and fascism. In that event, he preferred the latter. In October 1937 Lindbergh declared that Hitler's and Mussolini's regimes were the two "most virile nations in Europe today." In contrast to his praise of Nazi Germany, Lindbergh often condemned Western nations, including his own.

As a second world war loomed in Europe, opinions as explosive as these would soon lead to Lindbergh's fall from the status of national hero.

6

America First!

Horrified by the prospect of another and incomparably destructive European war, Lindbergh devoted himself to efforts to prevent the outbreak of conflict. He urged acquiescence to German eastward expansion in order to avoid conflict in the West. After Britain and France declared war on Germany in September 1939, however, Lindbergh focused his energies on opposing U.S. intervention in the war. That position brought him into direct conflict with the Roosevelt administration. Ultimately, Lindbergh's opposition to the war shattered his image as a national hero.

Just as Major Truman Smith had anticipated, Lindbergh's nine-day German tour in the summer of 1936 produced a wealth of information about Nazi air power. In the fall of 1937, Smith arranged for Lindbergh to return to the Third Reich for additional tours with his German hosts. Flying his own plane from Munich to Stuttgart, the aviator looked down in amazement at a seemingly unending series of Nazi airfields and military installations. By the end of his second tour he concluded that the Nazis would have the planes, trained pilots, and natural resources to overwhelm any European power in the air.

After completing the survey, Lindbergh collaborated with Smith in Berlin on a "General Estimate [of Germany's Air Power] of November 1, 1937." The report, officially submitted to the Army by Smith, but based on Lindbergh's findings, declared that "The astounding growth of German air power from a zero level to its present status in a brief four years must be accounted one of the most important world events of our time." Lindbergh estimated that German air power exceeded that of all European competitors and would reach parity with American military aviation by 1941 or 1942.

By now Lindbergh had become as enmeshed in analyzing air power and the explosive European diplomatic scene as he had been previously involved in commercial aviation and medical research. When he became interested in a subject, Lindbergh typically threw all of his energy into it. The threat of an incomparably destructive air war now obsessed him. He concluded that no European power could compete with the German war machine.

In order to test his suspicions about European air power, Lindbergh decided to follow up his two German tours by consulting American diplomats in Europe about the status of air power across the continent. Accompanied by Anne, he made survey trips to Poland, Romania, Czechoslovakia, and the Soviet Union. None impressed him, except the USSR, and it only in a negative way. "Russian life," he observed in 1938, "is as close to hell on earth as it is possible for human beings to come." He predicted "a collapse of the Russian system in the very near future." The fall of Soviet communism "might take several years but it is as much a certainty as anything of this type can be," he added. In any case, he was sure that Soviet air power would be no match for the Nazis. When Lindbergh's views about Russia leaked to the press, Soviet officials, who had lavished hospitality and entertainment on the aviation hero during his visit, bitterly denounced him. The Communist party newspaper *Pravda* branded him a "liar."

After he had completed his survey in mid–1938, Lindbergh believed that German air power exceeded that of all its European competitors *combined*. Accordingly, he concluded that Nazi aggression could not be stopped. Should England and France even attempt to ally with the USSR against Germany, they would be crushed in a horribly destructive European war that would kill millions and undermine all of Western civilization. Nothing was more important than heading off such a conflict.

Although the Army credited Lindbergh with heightening awareness of German air power, Lindbergh overestimated the prowess of the Luftwaffe. Beneath a fearsome facade, flaws plagued the Nazi air force and undermined its effectiveness in World War II. Prominent among those flaws was inept decision making on production decisions and use of air power, especially by Hitler himself.

At the time, however, the Luftwaffe appeared invincible to Lindbergh, who decried the contrasting weakness and lack of "virility" in the West. In May 1938, British diplomat Harold Nicolson, a Lindbergh family friend, described the aviator as "most pessimistic." Nicolson wrote in his diary that Lindbergh "believes in the Nazi theology, all tied up with his hatred of degeneracy and his hatred of democracy as represented by the free press and the American public." The publication of these words in Nicolson's diary in 1966 elicited a violent response from Lindbergh, who denied that he had embraced Nazi ideology.

In the fall of 1938 Lindbergh did gain the attention of the U.S. ambassador to Britain, Joseph P. Kennedy (father of the thirty-fifth U.S. president). After Kennedy forwarded a four-page letter from Lindbergh to the White House, military leaders in Washington reported that the aviator's information accorded "very closely" with their own estimates. By the fall of 1938 Western leaders, led by Britain's new prime minister, Neville Chamberlain, concluded that the only prudent course to avoid a general war in Europe was appeasement of Germany. Chamberlain, joined by the French and the Italians in a meeting with Hitler in Munich in late September, acquiesced to Hitler's annexation of the Sudetenland of Czechoslovakia. The Third Reich had already absorbed Austria in direct violation of the Versailles Treaty. At Munich Hitler promised that he would seek no further European expansion.

Shortly after the conference in Bavaria, Lindbergh received yet another invitation from Smith to journey to Berlin. There the American ambassador to Germany, Hugh Wilson, sought to take advantage of the hopeful diplomatic climate in the wake of Munich by hosting a dinner to honor Field Marshal Hermann Goering and Lindbergh. When the two honored guests greeted one another on October 18, Goering took out a red box, said a few words in German that Lindbergh did not understand, and "in the name of the führer" pinned on the aviator's chest the "Service Cross of the Order of the German Eagle with the Star," the second highest civilian medal and one intended expressly for foreigners. Although surprised, Lindbergh thought little of the incident and pocketed the medal, which he later sent to the Missouri Historical Society in St. Louis, where it joined most of the rest of the 171 medals he had received in the eleven years since his trans-Atlantic flight.

Later, when the medal ignited controversy, Major Smith explained that "Under the circumstances there was of course no possibility for Lindbergh to reject the decoration"—to have done so would have insulted both Wilson and Goering. Ambassador Wilson agreed, telling Lindbergh in 1941, "I have always felt that if you had refused the decoration . . . you would have been guilty of a breach of good taste." That night, however, when Lindbergh and Smith returned to the latter's apartment, Anne

Morrow Lindbergh took one look at the medal and said, "The albatross." Her words were prophetic.

About three weeks after the embassy dinner, the Nazis launched vicious anti-Jewish pogroms, prompting international condemnation. At the time, Lindbergh had actually begun making plans to move his family to Berlin. Still committed to doing what he could to avert war, the aviator explained that "The more difficult it is to have contact with [Germany] the more difficult an understanding will become. After all, contact does not necessarily mean support." Alexis Carrel joined other friends, however, in urging Lindbergh to abandon his plans, explaining that if he moved to Berlin he would lose his "moral authority" in the United States. The Lindberghs took an apartment in Paris instead. Lindbergh did not "give a damn" about how the public might view his actions, but he did "not wish to make a move which would seem to support the German actions in regard to the Jews."

Back in the United States, news of Lindbergh's acceptance of the Nazi medal and his consideration of moving the family to Berlin coincided with the outbreak of Nazi terrorism against German Jews. Harold Ickes, Roosevelt's secretary of interior, publicly attacked Lindbergh for accepting "a decoration at the hands of a brutal dictator who with that same hand is robbing and torturing thousands of fellow human beings." Editorial cartoons and telegrams called attention to what many interpreted as Lindbergh's pro-Nazi stance. The aviator, contemptuous of "pressmen" and public opinion, considered it a waste of his time to respond to such charges.

At the time Lindbergh busied himself with one final—and bizarre, under the circumstances—episode of the prewar period. He made two secret missions to Germany in behalf of the French government, which belatedly sought to bolster its weakness in air power by purchasing 300

German aircraft engines for French fighter planes. Still unwilling to believe the worst about his Nazi acquaintances, Lindbergh doggedly pursued the elusive deal, which fell through when in March 1939 Hitler broke his promise made at Munich by occupying the rest of Czechoslovakia.

Concluding that he had done all he could do in Europe, Lindbergh decided to return home. Rather than subject Anne and the children to the mob scene that would greet their arrival back in the United States, he decided to travel alone and have his family follow at a later date. When on April 8 his ship arrived in New York Harbor, the aviator had to fight his way with a police escort through scores of screaming reporters and aggressive photographers whose flashbulbs exploded with a puff of white smoke before his eyes. The incident did nothing to improve Lindbergh's perception of his native land. "It was a barbaric entry into a civilized country," he recalled.

Growing quickly nostalgic for the "privacy and decency" of Europe, Lindbergh, joined by his family, escaped briefly to Next Day Hill, the Morrow estate in New Jersey, before settling on Long Island. Determined to press his views on the European military situation, Lindbergh met with General H. H. "Hap" Arnold, chief of the Army Air Corps. Arnold, who had read Lindbergh's reports on German air power, credited the aviator with giving "the most accurate picture of the Luftwaffe, its equipment, leaders, apparent plans, training methods, and present defects." At Arnold's request, he placed himself on active duty at the rank of colonel in the Army Air Corps and initiated a review of American aeronautical research.

Spending much of his time in Washington, Lindbergh conferred with army and navy intelligence officials, Secretary of War Harry H. Woodring, members of Congress, and President Roosevelt himself. The president and the aviation hero chatted amiably in the Oval Office in their only meeting, which lasted fifteen minutes. Lindbergh recalled that he found FDR likable yet "too suave, too pleasant, too easy" and "did not trust" him. In fact, Roosevelt and Lindbergh were opposites that did not attract. The former loved politics, which the latter hated; FDR often acted precipitously and liked to "play it by ear," whereas Lindbergh rarely acted without careful and meticulous planning. Both were phenomenally successful men who had grown accustomed to achieving their aims while overcoming opposition. These differences, coupled with lingering resentment over the air mail controversy, formed the basis of a bitter rivalry between two of the most prominent Americans of their time.

Lindbergh found greater affinity of views with anti-New Deal conservatives such as Senator Harry F. Byrd of Virginia, radio commentator Fulton Lewis, Jr., and former State Department diplomat William Castle. In a dinner with Lewis and Castle on August 23, 1939, Lindbergh wondered whether it might be prudent to form an organization in opposition to U.S. involvement in any European war. Both Lewis and Castle expressed enthusiasm and encouraged Lindbergh to exploit his popularity to advance the cause of nonintervention. Lewis offered to set aside air time for Lindbergh should he choose to make a radio address. The aviator declined—for the time being.

By this time war in Europe was imminent. In August the Soviet Union stunned world opinion by signing a nonaggression pact with the Nazis. Under the agreement, the two powers divided Eastern Europe into spheres of influence. On September 3, two days after Hitler ordered an attack on western Poland, both England and France, having abandoned appeasement, declared war on Germany. As Lindbergh's worst fears—a war menacing Western civilization—began to be realized, he redoubled his determination to keep the United States out of the conflict.

Lindbergh now informed Lewis that he would like to accept his offer to provide air time for a radio address. "Much as I dislike taking part in politics and public life," he wrote privately, "I intend to do so if necessary to stop the trend which is now going on in this country." Lindbergh's plans for a radio address alarmed the Roosevelt administration. The president well knew from the air mail controversy that Lindbergh could be a powerful voice in national affairs. A sharply anti-interventionist speech by the popular hero would make it more difficult for Roosevelt to revise American neutrality legislation to make it possible to sell war material to Britain and France.

So anxious was Roosevelt to avoid conflict with Lindbergh over the European war that he decided to create a new Cabinet position, secretary of air, and offer it to the aviation hero. The offer, communicated to Lindbergh by Truman Smith, was contingent on Lindbergh calling off his radio address and avoiding public criticism of Roosevelt's European diplomacy. Lindbergh summarily rejected the offer, which served only to increase his contempt for politics in general and Roosevelt in particular.

Thus, the Roosevelt administration failed to head off Lindbergh's first public anti-interventionist speech, titled "America and European Wars," carried by all three nationwide radio networks on September 15. In his slightly high-pitched and nasal, but always clear and articulate, voice, Lindbergh declared that "the destiny of this country does not call for our involvement in European wars." He predicted that if the United States began aiding the Allies, it would soon be compelled to fight with them, and might "lose a million men, possibly several million." The country would also assume costly obligations that would endure years beyond the fighting of the war itself. Meanwhile, the demands of war would undermine freedom at home. "If we enter fighting for democracy abroad," he averred, "we may end by losing it at home." The aviation expert assured his audience that the United States, taking advantage of its natural ocean boundaries, ideal for defensive warfare, could best assure its own security by remaining a nonbelligerent.

This first speech, heard by millions of Americans, established the major themes that Lindbergh would reiterate throughout his anti-interventionist campaign. His advocacy of strict neutrality won both praise and bitter condemnation from politicians, journalists, and the public. His second address, "Neutrality and War," followed in October, eliciting an even greater reaction. Lindbergh also began publishing anti-intervention articles and speeches in such popular journals as *Reader's Digest, Atlantic Monthly,* and *Collier's.* He insisted that Nazi expansionist ambitions focused on Eastern Europe; hence Britain and France should seek a negotiated settlement. A war among Great Britain, France, and Germany would only serve to weaken all three, to the benefit of Russia and Japan.

Lindbergh offered a racialist—and racist—argument in support of nonintervention. Writing in *Reader's Digest* in November 1939, he declared that war would "reduce the strength and destroy the treasures of the White race" and might "even lead to the end of our Civilization." The real threat to Western interests, he asserted, came from the east in the form of Soviet communism and the masses of Asia. Perhaps recalling his own harrowing experience when hungry villagers attempted to board his plane during flood relief efforts in China, Lindbergh sounded the alarm about the "pressing sea of Yellow, Black, and Brown." Instead of fighting a war in Europe, it was now time "to build our White ramparts again." Lindbergh's simplistic views on race were common at the time in the United States, where rigid racial segregation prevailed.

Although Lindbergh never shared his father's passion for excoriating the rich and defending the interests of the "common man," he now recalled the fight against U.S. entry in World War I. "I am certainly aware that there is much of my father in me," Lindbergh observed. C. A. Lindbergh's Minnesota rivals had vilified him as a "Gopher Bolshevist" for his campaign against U.S. intervention in the Great War. The son would now endure the wrath of interventionists as well.

By the fall of 1939 Charles Lindbergh had established himself as the most controversial opponent of the European war. As a result of his repeated vists to Germany and his outspokenness, Lindbergh already was called a "fascist," "spy," and a "rat" in Paris, London, and in some circles in the United States. In 1939 TWA dropped "The Lindbergh Line" slogan from its annual promotional literature. However, prominent Republican noninterventionists such as former president Hoover, Hiram Johnson of California, and William Borah of Idaho congratulated and encouraged Lindbergh. Borah, former chairman of the Senate Foreign Relations Committee, even suggested that the aviator seek the Republican nomination in order to challenge Roosevelt for the presidency in 1940, an idea that Lindbergh quickly rejected.

Anne Morrow Lindbergh contributed a more philosophical dissent on world affairs. After Charles began speaking out, she wrote a small book that provoked a large controversy. Titled *The Wave of the Future,* it became an immediate best-seller in 1940. Anne argued that fascist aggression stemmed from the frustrations of World War I. While she found fascism and communism abhorrent, those social systems had provided a means of reconciling the "great material advance" of modern society, which had come at "the expense of moral and spiritual" values. Fascism and communism represented the "scum on the wave of the future." Rather than intervening in the war, which would "only add to the chaos," Anne advised a traditional policy of nonentanglement combined with efforts to improve American domestic life. Critics accused Anne of undermining democracy as well as her own father's legacy.

Public opinion polls at the time revealed, however, that most Americans shared the Lindberghs' desire for the United States to remain neutral in the European war. A substantial number of Americans believed that their country had intervened in World War I, not to make the world "safe for democracy," as President Wilson had intoned, but rather because of the greed of bankers and munitions makers who had profited from the conflict. Many Americans now interpreted Roosevelt's efforts to aid the Allies as first steps toward direct intervention in another European war.

Events of the spring of 1940, however, began to reshape American public opinion. With brutal efficiency, the Nazi *blitzkrieg* ("lightning war") overwhelmed Denmark, Norway, Belgium, and Holland, then circumvented the supposedly impregnable Maginot Line en route to Paris. As France capitulated and Hitler launched the Battle of Britain, Roosevelt, deciding to run for an unprecedented third term, won support for his effort to aid the Allies short of direct U.S. intervention. The president had encouraged the activities of various preparedness and interventionist groups, the most prominent being the Committee to Defend America by Aiding the Allies. In response, in September 1940 noninterventionists, led by Sears, Roebuck chairman General Robert E. Wood and R. Douglas Stuart, a twenty-four-year-old law student, organized the rival America First Committee.

Following his reelection, FDR precipitated an intense battle with noninterventionists—including Lindbergh—over his proposed "lend-lease" program, announced to the nation on January 6, 1941. The president insisted that the United States did not have to enter the war, but could serve as the "great arsenal for democracy" by providing extensive material support for the Allied war effort. Noninterventionists rejected as duplicitous Roosevelt's argument that lend-lease would make U.S. intervention less rather than more likely. Congressional hearings on lend-lease set the stage for a bitter confrontation between Roosevelt and the noninterventionists.

Lindbergh took center stage, appearing before both House and Senate committees, as the debate unfolded. The aviator was not opposed to supplying Britain and France with defensive weapons, but he undermined Roosevelt's depiction of lend-lease as the first line of *American* defense. The prospect of an eventual German air attack on the United States, Lindbergh argued, was remote. By the time of his congressional testimony in February 1941, Britain had not only survived the Nazi aerial assault, but had also inflicted severe damage on the Luftwaffe, which Lindbergh himself had once viewed as all-powerful. If Britain, in much closer proximity to Germany, could fend off the Luftwaffe, he explained, the United States had little to fear from it. Lindbergh asserted that lend-lease would "lead to failure in war, and to conditions in our own country as bad or worse than those we now desire to overthrow in Nazi Germany." The aviator advocated strict U.S. neutrality backed by a strong defense, including a two-ocean navy, and called for a prompt declaration of war against any nation that sought to establish a military presence in the Americas.

Although Lindbergh, ever the lone eagle, preferred to operate independently, he began to see the advantages of working with others to keep the United States out of the war. By the time of the lend-lease debate he had met or corresponded with virtually every significant anti-interventionist figure in the country. As the political struggle between the Roosevelt administration and the noninterventionists intensified, on April 17, 1941, Lindbergh joined the national committee of the America First Committee. He had already been aiding the organization informally, but had declined Wood's offer that he serve as national chairman. America First was easily the largest anti-interventionist group, which by the time of Pearl Harbor consisted of 450 chapters and subchapters involving a total national membership of 800,000 to 850,000 persons. Lindbergh gave the committee an immediate boost, becoming its most popular national speaker and spurring recruitment of new members.

Four days before Lindbergh's first scheduled public address as a member of America First, the Roosevelt administration launched a public campaign to discredit him. Once again, the front man for the attack was Secretary of Interior Harold Ickes. In a speech on April 13, Ickes called Lindbergh the "No. 1 Nazi fellow traveler" in the United States and "the proud possessor of a Nazi decoration which has already been well earned." He described Anne's book, *The Wave of the Future,* as "the bible of every American Nazi, Fascist, and appeaser."

There can be no doubt that Ickes's brutal attack was part of a calculated administration effort to discredit the leading spokesman of the noninterventionist opposition. In May 1940 Roosevelt himself told Treasury Secretary Henry Morgenthau, Jr., "I am absolutely convinced that Lindbergh is a Nazi." On several occasions the president and his Cabinet discussed ways to combat "the appeasement movement." Lindbergh's name figured prominently in those discussions. The FBI amassed a bulky file on Lindbergh's statements, foreign connections, and finances. The bureau also tapped his telephone, prompting Lindbergh to tell his friends to speak up so that they could be heard clearly. He also offered to open his own files to federal investigators and respond to any questions they might pose. The IRS investigated his finances and those of other anti-interventionists. Roosevelt supporters such as Senators James F. Byrnes, Key Pittman, and Claude Pepper joined Ickes in questioning Lindbergh's character.

Normally, Lindbergh ignored public criticism, but Ickes had challenged his patriotism. The aviation hero responded in a letter to Roosevelt in which he resigned his commission as a colonel in the Army Air Corps, explaining that he had "no honorable alternative" since FDR, his commander-in-chief, had questioned his loyalty through Ickes's attack. Lindbergh submitted his resignation "with the utmost regret," explaining that membership in the Air Corps was "one of the things that has meant most to me in my life." Privately, he reflected unhappily on the irony of a situation that found him "stumping the country with pacifists and . . . resigning as a colonel in the Army Air Corps, when there is no philosophy I disagree with more than that of the pacifist, and nothing I would rather be doing than flying in the Air Corps."

Despite such laments in his journal, Lindbergh became even more strongly committed to expressing his noninterventionist views. He attracted an enthusiastic crowd of 10,000 in his inaugural America First address in Chicago on April 17, while thousands more strained to hear him outside. Thunderous applause greeted his next appearance in New York, by which time requests for a "Lindbergh rally" poured into America First headquarters. In his speeches, each carefully prepared by his own hand, Lindbergh sharpened his criticisms of the president for exceeding his constitutional authority by leading the country step-by-step toward war. Typical was a speech in Philadelphia on May 29 in which Lindbergh declaimed: "Mr. Roosevelt claims that Hitler desires to dominate the world. But it is Mr. Roosevelt himself who advocates world domination when he says that it is our business to control the wars of Europe and Asia, and that we in America must dominate islands lying off the African coast."

A critical turning point in World War II—the Nazi invasion of Russia on June 22, 1941—strengthened Lindbergh's anti-interventionist convictions. Hitler's invasion of the USSR confirmed Lindbergh's long-held insistence that Nazi ambitions lay in the East rather than the West. "Intervention by England and France in the war between Germany and Poland did not save Poland," Lindbergh asserted on July 1, 1941. Western intervention had merely "postponed the war between Germany and Russia, and brought the defeat of France and the devastation of England." Moreover, Japan, which in September 1940 signed the Tripartite Pact with Italy and Germay, had now been driven "into the arms of the Axis."

The outbreak of fighting between Germany and the USSR also increased Lindbergh's contempt for American interventionists who sought to depict the conflict as a struggle between democracy and tyranny. He expressed amazement that "The idealists who have been shouting against the horrors of Nazi Germany are now ready to welcome Soviet Russia as an ally." How could those who promoted intervention on a moral basis be "ready to join with a nation whose record of cruelty, bloodshed, and barbarism" was, he asserted, "without parallel in modern history"? Nazi Germany itself would be a more fit ally than the Soviets, Lindbergh insisted.

Despite such arguments, the Roosevelt administration welcomed the Soviet Union into the Allied coalition and redoubled its efforts to discredit Lindbergh. Harold Ickes, who had been compiling a thick file on the aviator's activities, still led the charge. "No one has ever heard Lindbergh utter a word of horror at, or even aversion to, the bloody career that the Nazis are following," the secretary of interior declared on July 14, 1941. Ickes had "never heard this Knight of the German Eagle denounce Hitler or nazism or Mussolini or fascism." While the aviator did nothing to bolster the cause of democracy, "All of Lindbergh's passion-ate words are to encourage Hitler and to break down the will of his own fellow citizens to resist Hitler and nazism."

The continuing references to the medal Lindbergh had received from Goering finally prompted a public response. He had refrained from making any statement about the medal because he wished to avoid getting into "a child's spitting contest" over what he considered a trivial matter. Ickes called attention to Lindbergh's receipt of the German decoration because the incident linked the aviator to the Nazi regime. Lindbergh, however, insisted that the medal merely provided his opponents with a convenient symbol on which to base attacks on his character. If he had never received the medal, he averred, they would have found some other basis on which to attack him. He would not reward those who sought to sully his reputation by renouncing the medal or sending it back, as some of his friends advised him to do.

Lindbergh did decide, however, that Ickes's continuing efforts to use the Goering medal to call into question his patriotism were sufficient cause for another letter to Roosevelt. On July 16, 1941, the aviator reminded the president that he received the German decoration "in the American Embassy, in the presence of your Ambassador," and that he "was there at his request in order to assist in creating a better relationship between the American Embassy and the German Government." Lindbergh asserted the he had "a right to an apology" for Ickes's impugnment of his patriotism, since he had no connection or contacts with any foreign governments since leaving Europe in 1939. Noting that Lindbergh had released his letter to the press, Roosevelt's press secretary said that it had been written for public relations purposes and that no White House response or apology would be forthcoming.

The ongoing public confrontation between Roosevelt and Lindbergh encouraged speculation that the aviator would enter the political arena. Lindbergh, however, declared that he had "little interest in either politics or popularity." When friends and advisers argued that he could not avoid being swept into a campaign for political office, he replied that he could do so simply "by making one address, or by writing one article in which I discuss truthfully and openly the fundamental issues which face the country today." Lindbergh declared that "One of the dearest of rights to me is being able to say what I think and act as I wish. I intend to do this, and I know it will cause trouble. As soon as it does, the politicians will disown me quickly enough—and I will be only too willing."

The words were prophetic. Politicians, and many others, would in fact disown Lindbergh as a result of his controversial statements. Some of Lindbergh's fellow anti-interventionists, including William Castle, historian Charles Beard, and socialist Norman Thomas, warned Lindbergh that he should alter the tone of his speeches. They explained that he would win a wider following if he made more effort to condemn Nazi cruelty and hold out more hope for the courageous resistance of the British and the other enemies of fascism. But Lindbergh was more interested in plain speaking than the art of public relations. He told his colleagues that he wrote his speeches "without any attempt to gain popularity and with the feeling that it is desirable for someone to speak frankly and as he actually feels." Lindbergh occasionally condemned Nazi atrocities, yet years later he recalled that in the pre-Pearl Harbor period it had become "such a fetish to damn the enemy that I got disgusted with it."

Lindbergh was the most vilified of the anti-interventionists. He received death and kidnapping threats as well as mail addressed to "Dear Nazi Lindbergh." The interventionist group Friends of Democracy published a twenty-eight-page pamphlet titled, "Is Lindbergh a Nazi?" Foes suggested that he be deported to Germany. Charlotte, North Carolina, changed a street name from Lindbergh Avenue to Avon Drive. New York's Lafayette Hotel, owned by Raymond Orteig, took down the banner honoring Lindbergh's solo flight and his receipt of the 1927 Orteig Prize.

Undaunted, Lindbergh continued his antiwar campaign. He had not turned back when he encountered ice storms during his 1927 solo flight over the Atlantic; neither would he do so now. Not wishing to rehash the same speech, Lindbergh worked on a new address in which he meant to pinpoint which groups supported American intervention in the war and why they did so. For months Lindbergh had resisted naming names and organizations because he hoped "it would not be necessary to do this." But by the fall of 1941, with Roosevelt becoming increasingly bold in efforts to provoke an incident that would build popular support for U.S. belligerence, Lindbergh saw intervention as "practically inevitable." Before war came, he wished to "name the groups responsible for pushing us into it."

Lindbergh knew that his speech in Des Moines, Iowa, on September 11, titled "Who Are the War Agitators?", would be the most controversial of all his America First addresses. More than 8,000 persons appeared at the Des Moines Coliseum—"the most unfriendly crowd of any to date," Lindbergh recalled—on the home ground of interventionist FDR Cabinet member Henry A. Wallace. Just before the America First speakers appeared, the audience listened to Roosevelt's national broadcast reporting on clashes in the North Atlantic between American and German warships. The president misrepresented the September 4 incident involving the U.S. destroyer *Greer* as an unprovoked attack, when in fact the United States had precipitated the clash. Lindbergh faced "a unique and difficult situation" in trying to appeal to a crowd that the president, a skilled orator, had just rallied in support of an alleged unprovoked attack on the American flag.

Never one to shirk a challenge, Lindbergh plunged in, telling the audience that he intended to speak "with the utmost frankness" about those who were "responsible for changing our national policy from one of neutrality and independence to one of entanglement in European affairs." According to Lindbergh, "The three most important groups who have been pressing this country toward war are the British, the Jewish, and the Roosevelt Administration." Intellectuals, finance capitalists, Communists (since the Nazi attack on Russia in June 1941), and other groups also promoted intervention, but Lindbergh focused on the three major groups of "war agitators." Although they represented "only a small minority of our people," the three interventionist groups skillfully employed "misinformation" and "propaganda," to convince "sincere but misguided men and women to follow their lead." The interventionists had masked their step-by-step campaign to lead the nation into war, initially by calling for preparedness and later by trying to provoke an incident with Germany. All along the way, Lindbergh added, they had conducted a "smear campaign" against noninterventionists.

The reaction to Lindbergh's speech focused almost exclusively on his reference to Jews. Thereafter, the only public reference Lindbergh made regarding Jews would tar him with a reputation for anti-Semitism. In fact, Lindbergh's wartime journals reveal that Nazi anti-Semitism bothered him, and shook the foundations of his respect for certain aspects of German culture. In his Des Moines address, Lindbergh criticized Jews the least, and the Roosevelt administration the most, of the three groups he blamed for inciting U.S. intervention. The aviator declared that "No person with a sense of the dignity of mankind can condone the persecution of the Jewish race [sic] in Germany." While Lindbergh insisted that he did not "blame [Jews] for looking out for what they believe to be their own interests," Americans should not "allow the natural passions and prejudices of other peoples to lead our country to destruction."

Although Jewish-Americans were a significant and largely interventionist interest group in national politics on the eve of World War II, Lindbergh exaggerated their influence and subscribed to stereotypical views. Jews were neither a separate "race" nor people "other" than Americans. Since August 1939, when he discussed the issue with William Castle and Fulton Lewis, Jr., Lindbergh had been "disturbed about the effect of the Jewish influence in our press, radio, and motion pictures." Given the context of the times, with the Nazi regime conducting organized pogroms against Jews, Lindbergh's comments, easily equated with virulent anti-Semitism, were ill-advised at best. When Anne read an advance copy of the speech, she erupted, "You can't say that!"

In handwritten drafts of the Des Moines speech, Lindbergh wrote that he knew he would be attacked, but made his explosive comments anyway. "I realize that tomorrow morning's headlines will say, 'Lindbergh Attacks Jews.' The ugly cry of anti-Semitism . . . will be waved about my name. It is so much simpler to brand someone with a bad label than to take the trouble to read what he says." Lindbergh accurately anticipated the predominant reaction. The vast majority of newspaper commentaries proved sharply critical. "The voice is the voice of Lindbergh," declared the *San Francisco Chronicle*, in the most stinging rebuke, "but the words are the words of Hitler." Roosevelt's spokesman gleefully seized the opportunity, observing that "a striking similarity" existed between Lindbergh's speech and Nazi propaganda.

While Lindbergh could easily anticipate the administration's response, the reaction of his colleagues in the America First Committee came as a surprise. Norman Thomas dropped out of the organization after Lindbergh's address, explaining that while much of what the aviation hero said was true, and that criticism of the speech was "insincere and hypocritical," U.S. intervention in the war would have come regardless of Jewish influence. Noting that Lindbergh had done "great harm" to the cause, Thomas observed that it was "an enormous pity that our friend the Colonel will not take the advice on public relations which he would expect an amateur in aviation to take from an expert." Noninterventionist Senator Robert A. Taft condemned the aviator for referring "to the Jews as if they were a foreign race, and not Americans at all." Nevertheless, Taft added, whatever intolerance Lindbergh displayed had been "more than matched" by the intolerance others had shown toward his views.

Some, like anti-interventionist Senator Gerald P. Nye, defended Lindbergh, insisting that "the Jewish people are a large factor in our movement toward war." Others pointed out that Lindbergh's words had been taken out of context. Some noted that the leading interventionist groups included prominent members who actually *practiced* anti-Semitism through their membership in social clubs that excluded Jews. After reviewing Lindbergh's speech, the America First leadership declined to repudiate him or accept his offer to disassociate his views from the organization.

Lindbergh himself retracted nothing and saw no reason for apology or clarification. As always, he had chosen his words carefully and had said precisely what he had wished to say. He insisted that reporters had distorted his speech; that most Jews advocated U.S. intervention; and that "You should not hide reality." Despite his defense,

Lindbergh's comments had encouraged anti-Semitism, divided the noninterventionist movement, and sullied his own reputation.

Worst of all, from Lindbergh's own point of view, the aspect of the Des Moines speech that received the least attention was that which he had emphasized most: the Roosevelt administration's efforts to maneuver the country into war. The aviator focused almost exclusively on that theme in his remaining America First addresses. Speaking in Fort Wayne, Indiana, on October 3, Lindbergh asserted that "Not one step the Administration has taken in the last two years was placed honestly before our people as a step toward war." In his final America First address, before 20,000 people in New York's Madison Square Garden six weeks before the Japanese attack on Pearl Harbor, Lindbergh called for "a leadership of integrity instead of subterfuge, of openness instead of secrecy."

Few, including Lindbergh, anticipated a Japanese attack on Pearl Harbor, although the Pacific war itself came as no surprise since the United States "had been prodding them into war for weeks." After December 7, 1941, America First promptly ceased distributing its literature, canceled its rallies, and called for all Americans to support the war. The day after Pearl Harbor, Lindbergh issued a statement calling for unity "regardless of our attitude in the past toward the policy our government has followed." The nation had been "attacked by force of arms, and by force of arms we must retaliate." He called on the whole country to "now turn every effort toward building the greatest and most efficient Army, Navy, and Air Force in the world." Noting in his journal that "all that I feared would happen has happened," Lindbergh prepared to witness "the bloodiest and most devastating war of all history."

7

After the Fall

World War II marked a turning point in Lindbergh's life, one that matched the impact of his epic New York-to-Paris flight. Vilified by the Roosevelt administration and scorned by much of the public, Lindbergh lost his status as a national hero. The fall from grace was actually a welcome development, one that Lindbergh had done much to bring on himself. Much to his relief in the war and postwar years, the press and public paid him dramatically less attention than they had before.

Like the overwhelming majority of patriotic Americans, Lindbergh sought to serve his country during the war. Although the United States had, in his view, provoked Japan through its economic sanctions and diplomatic confrontation, Lindbergh saw no alternative to war after Pearl Harbor. "If I had been in Congress," he wrote in his journal on December 8, "I certainly would have voted for a declaration of war."

When the aviator tried to reenlist in the Army Air Corps after the outbreak of war, however, the Roosevelt administration vindictively obstructed his path. As always, Harold Ickes led the campaign against Lindbergh. On December 20, 1941, the Secretary of the Interior told FDR that his analysis of a "complete indexed collection" of Lindbergh's speeches left him convinced that the aviator was "a ruthless and conscious fascist" who should not be allowed to serve in the U.S. armed forces. The president promptly responded that he agreed "wholeheartedly" with Ickes's assessment.

Unaware of the administration's intentions, Lindbergh traveled to Washington in mid-January in a quest for an active role in the war. William Donovan, head of the Office of Strategic Services (precursor to the postwar CIA), offered Lindbergh a position in his organization—if the administration would approve—but the aviator wanted to serve in the Army Air Corps. When Lindbergh attempted to meet with General H. H. Arnold, however, he was advised to discuss the matter directly with Secretary of War Henry Stimson. When the two men met on January 12, Stimson commended Lindbergh for the "really valuable service" rendered by his reports on German aviation and military power, but also called attention to the aviator's prewar "political views" and "lack of aggressiveness" toward the nation's current enemies. Stimson told Lindbergh directly that he was "unwilling to place in command of our troops as a commissioned officer any man who had such a lack of faith in our cause, as he had shown in his speeches."

Had Lindbergh been willing to make a public statement repudiating his prewar views, the path may have been cleared for his return to service in the Army Air Corps. Lindbergh rejected such a course as expedient and stood by his pre-Pearl Harbor opposition to U.S. intervention. The day after meeting with Stimson, Lindbergh told Arnold and Assistant Secretary of War Robert Lovett that he had no intention of retracting his earlier views. Although Lindbergh expressed "very little confidence" in Roosevelt's leadership, he would, should he be allowed to serve, remain loyal to the president in his role as commander-in-chief. This position proved unacceptable. The meeting ended with agreement that it would be best for all concerned if Lindbergh performed his wartime service in the commercial aviation industry.

Accordingly, Lindbergh contacted his longtime friend and business associate, Pan American Airways executive Juan Trippe, who expressed his eagerness to gain Lindbergh's services to help manage the increased demands of wartime production. Days later, however, Trippe telephoned Lindbergh to inform him that "obstacles had been put in the way" and that his offer to join the team at Pan Am had to be withdrawn. The same scenario played out when Lindbergh contacted his longtime associates at United Airlines and Curtiss-Wright. In both cases the corporation would have welcomed Lindbergh's services, but when the executives checked with the War Department and the White House to determine whether there would be any objections they learned that it would be inexpedient to employ Lindbergh.

Dejected, Lindbergh confronted the possibility that he would "be blocked in every attempt I make to take part in this war." Even though he still predicted that U.S. involvement ultimately would prove to be "foolish and disastrous," Lindbergh was a patriotic man of action who badly wanted to serve his country in a time of national peril. "I have always believed in the past that every American citizen had the right and the duty to state his opinion in peace and to fight for his country in war," he explained. "But the Roosevelt Administration seems to think otherwise."

Fortunately for Lindbergh, one man in the United States had the power and contempt for national political authority to offer the aviator an opportunity to take part in the war effort. Henry Ford had admired Lindbergh since the young aviator had given the industrialist his first airplane ride in 1927. Ford had already contracted with the War Department to produce B-24 four-engine bombers at his new Willow Run factory, set up for that purpose. In March 1942 Ford summoned Lindbergh to Detroit and offered him a role in the bomber production program. Neither the War Department nor the White House opposed the appointment, recognizing that Ford was too powerful to challenge.

Lindbergh promptly accepted Ford's offer to become a technical consultant at the Willow Run bomber plant. Although Lindbergh was almost forty years younger than Ford, the two men held certain characteristics in common. Both were mechanical geniuses who believed in hard work and clean living (neither smoked nor drank). Both had opposed the war and expressed contempt for Roosevelt. Both had identifed Jews as supporters of American involvement in Europe's wars. Ford, however, had been far more extreme on the subject than Lindbergh, particularly in the early 1920s when his newspaper, the *Dearborn Independent,* ran a series of virulently anti-Semitic diatribes.

With the war escalating in Europe and Asia, however, there was little time for talk about anything other than the pressing business of bomber production. Glad to have found a niche at last, Lindbergh expressed relief that he could devote himself to "technical fields" in his work at Willow Run. Keeping opinions to himself, he made no public statements about political matters during the war. His work gave Lindbergh regular opportunities to spend time with his mother, who still lived in Detroit. Anne and the rest of the family joined the aviation expert in their new residence in an exclusive Detroit suburb. As a result of their prewar views, the Lindberghs found themselves shunned socially, even to the point of being disinvited to parties as a result of complaints by other guests, some of whom considered Lindbergh an anti-Semite. Lindbergh paid less attention to the social ostracism than Anne, who had also briefly put aside her writing as a result of the intense criticism heaped on *The Wave of the Future.* Anne devoted herself to motherhood, bearing her fifth child, Scott, in 1942 and accommodated her spare time by taking up sculpture.

Working long days and often nights at Willow Run, Lindbergh expressed sharp dissatisfaction over the organization of the bomber production program at the plant. He encountered myriad frustrations accommodating Ford's eccentric style of industrial management as well as periodic interference from U.S. military advisers, whom he considered incompetent on aeronautics. Had it not been for his strong personal relationship with Ford and his belief that his work aided the war effort, Lindbergh would not long have remained at Willow Run. As it turned out, however, his organizational skill proved instrumental in helping to get B-24 bomber production underway. Pleased by the example of rapid progress in the wartime production campaign, Roosevelt paid a secret visit to the Willow Run plant in September 1942. Lindbergh marked the occasion by taking a rare day off. He and the president remained bitter, but distant, enemies.

Always eager for new challenges, Lindbergh joined a group of pilots at the Mayo Clinic in his native Minnesota to serve as a guinea pig in testing cockpit conditions for wartime aviators. Still in excellent physical condition at age forty-one, Lindbergh put himself through wrenching trials on the effects of air pressure at high altitude. The tests included having volunteers breathe pure oxygen while exercising on a treadmill (thereby removing nitrogen from the body), then entering a pressure tank that simulated altitudes up to 45,000 feet. Lindbergh would spend as long as three hours in the pressure tanks as his body temperature was raised and lowered so that the effects could be monitored. On one occasion, a tube jammed, cutting off Lindbergh's oxygen, briefly causing him to pass out.

By 1943 the exigencies of war had blurred memories of the prewar battles over intervention. As a result, Lindbergh no longer encountered opposition in his efforts to serve in other war industries. Still affiliated with Ford, Lindbergh now became a consultant with United Aircraft in its production of the F-4U Corsair single-seat fighter plane in Stratford, Connecticut. Lindbergh used the position to assume a combat role in the Pacific War.

In April 1944 the aviator made his way to the South Pacific. He stopped at marine bases en route to observe the Corsair in operation, noting the requirements for a more advanced fighter plane. After spending a few weeks monitoring the planes, and reef diving in his spare time, Lindbergh managed to get a Corsair assigned to him personally. Having his own wings allowed Lindbergh to engage in far more than observing and consulting.

Over the next few months he flew fifty combat missions against the Japanese. His activities ran the entire gamut: he engaged in patrols, reconnaissance, escort, strafing missions, and dive bombing. While the younger pilots were thrilled to have the legendary Lone Eagle flying in formation, officials in Washington knew nothing about it. Lindbergh kept them, and any Japanese who might be monitoring enemy radio communications, in the dark about his real identity by using the unimaginative alias of Jones in his airborne communications.

When word leaked out that the fabled conqueror of the Atlantic was flying combat missions as a civilian, in defiance of military regulations, General George C. Kenney summoned Lindbergh to General Douglas MacArthur's headquarters in Brisbane, Australia. Lindbergh had already met the generals, both of whom admired him. On the other hand, as Kenney explained, "It would raise one hell of a hullabaloo if you were shot down." Kenney speculated that because Lindbergh was a civilian, he would have his "head chopped off" by the Japanese if he was captured during a combat mission.

Lindbergh persuaded the generals to look the other way while he continued to fly in fighter planes. The three men then discussed ways to increase fuel efficiency before Lindbergh returned to the combat zone. The decision to continue flying combat missions nearly cost Lindbergh his life. On July 28 he engaged a Japanese Sonia-type fighter in an aerial dogfight. The two planes missed colliding by only a few feet as they roared toward each other, guns blazing, at 500 miles an hour. Lindbergh inflicted a kill, sending the Japanese plane spiraling into the sea below.

Three days later, however, a Japanese Zero surprised him from behind and had the aviation hero clearly in its sights. Lindbergh braced himself for death, thinking of Anne and the children, but the Japanese pilot inexplicably missed at close range. Lindbergh had always considered his aviation feats the result of careful planning, but on this occasion he would admit that he deserved the moniker "Lucky Lindy."

In part because of his racist views about the "yellow peril," Lindbergh believed more in the Pacific War than he did in the fight against Germany, which, despite Nazism, he considered ultimately a "civilized" nation. For these reasons, the aviator had no moral qualms about engaging in combat, except for bombing civilian targets, which bothered him greatly. He could revel in a dogfight, or in precision bombing of Japanese military facilities, but considered the destruction of unseen civilians little short of dishonorable. In a gripping passage of his wartime memoirs, Lindbergh recalled a moment when he released his hand from the trigger after sighting onto a man striding across the beach in a shoot-on-sight zone. Impressed by the courage of the man, who disdained to run from the American fighter plane, Lindbergh concluded that "His life is worth more than the pressure of a trigger. . . . I am glad I have not killed him. I would never have forgotten him writhing on the beach."

By mid-August 1944 word had circulated throughout New Guinea (although it had not reached the United States) that Lindbergh had engaged the "Japs" in two aerial dogfights. General Kenney decided the time had come to ground the Lone Eagle, informing him that it would be best for all concerned if Lindbergh focused his energies on teaching pilots fuel economy. "If anyone could fly a little monoplane from New York to Paris and have gas left over," Kenney reasoned, "he ought to be able to teach my P-38 pilots how to get more range out of their planes." MacArthur promptly approved the proposal to send Lindbergh from the air to the airfield classroom to instruct pilots in fuel conservation. Always enthusiastic about aircraft efficiency, Lindbergh taught hundreds of pilots how to "rev down" their engines and use a less rich mixture to save fuel. He also found time to conduct experiments in carrying heavier bomb loads.

Completing his service in the South Pacific, Lindbergh returned on September 20, 1944, to join his family in their new home on the Connecticut shore. He continued to act as a consultant with Ford and United Aircraft for the duration of the war. In mid-May 1945, little more than a week after the Nazi surrender, Lindbergh returned to Germany as a United civilian consultant to the U.S. Naval Technical Mission to report on German developments in aircraft and missiles. The trip provided an opportunity to see firsthand the devastation of Europe, which only confirmed in Lindbergh's mind his long-held view that the war would destroy Western civilization. While touring Munich he saw "mile after mile of bombed and ruined buildings, high piles of rubble where God knows how many people died or how many bodies still lie buried."

The American victory had come at relatively low cost—fewer than 400,000 Americans died of a total of 35 million soldiers and civilians who perished in the conflict—but Lindbergh had not abandoned his position that World War II had been a tragic mistake in which the United States should have taken no part. To most Americans, victory in the global conflict had proven the merits of American democracy and had vaulted the nation to a position of world power. The war thus confirmed in their minds the venerable notion, older than the Republic itself, that the United States was an exceptional nation, morally superior to others and destined to lead. Lindbergh did not share this view and frequently commented on the hypocrisy of American exceptionalism.

While the press and public depicted the "Japs" as barbaric perpetrators of wartime atrocities, Lindbergh had seen enough in the Pacific and Europe to convince him that atrocities were "not a thing confined to any nation or to any people. . . . It was freely admitted," he wrote in his wartime journal, that some Americans tortured prisoners and "were as cruel and barbaric at times as the Japs themselves. Our men think nothing of shooting a Japanese prisoner or a soldier attempting to surrender." Americans called "screaming" attention to Japanese atrocities "while we cover up our own and condone them as just retribution."

Lindbergh disapproved of early postwar proscriptions against fraternization with Germans, condemning the arrogance with which American soldiers treated the defeated enemy. His wartime memoirs made it clear that he blamed Hitler and the Nazi elite for Europe's destruction, but he counted the German people among their victims.

Still not recognizing the horrible uniqueness of the Holocaust—the coldly calculated genocide of European Jewry and other minorities—Lindbergh wrongly concluded that "What Germany has done to the Jew in Europe, we are doing to the Jap in the Pacific." The United States had bombed—and bombed excessively—both German and Japanese civilian targets, a process culminating with the atomic attacks on Hiroshima and Nagasaki in August 1945. But however horrific such destruction was, it differed from Nazi genocide, an important distinction that Lindbergh failed to grasp.

Lindbergh was a patriot, but in his view the unnecessary war had not increased American national security. Instead, it had resulted in the destruction of Germany, thus leading to the extension of the even more objectionable Soviet power into the heart of Europe. His combat experience in the South Pacific convinced Lindbergh that the United States had won the war only because of the superiority of American industry and military hardware. Accordingly, the Cold War perception of a global Communist threat emanating from Moscow made Lindbergh a staunch advocate of American preparedness. Indeed, he always had been, but in the prewar period he drew a sharp distinction between preparedness and intervention.

Whereas Lindbergh's opposition to U.S. intervention had made him an outsider from 1939–1941, his uncompromising anti-communism and support for increased American military power became mainstream views in the Cold War. Air power had been a crucial component of the victorious wartime strategy and Lindbergh, as one of the world's foremost aviation experts, was much in demand to assist in the formulation of American Cold War military strategy. The death of Roosevelt in April 1945 had removed the last obstacle in the path of Lindbergh's rehabilitation. Although he was no longer a dashing young hero, Lindbergh served as a consensus figure in the Cold War military establishment.

As a member of the Air Force Scientific Advisory Board, a committee that emerged as a result of the creation of the Air Force as an independent branch of the military service in 1947, Lindbergh traveled frequently to secret proving grounds in New Mexico to monitor tests. He consulted with Wernher von Braun and other German scientists brought to the United States as architects of postwar rocket research. When the Soviet Union attempted to block Western access to jointly occupied Berlin, lying within the Soviet sphere of eastern Germany, Lindbergh became a consultant on the airlift of 1948–1949. He helped devise plans to fly supplies in to the Western sectors of Berlin and rode as a passenger several times through the air corridor over eastern Germany.

Lindbergh spent most of his time as a key consultant to the Strategic Air Command (SAC). In the winter of 1948–1949 he flew around the world (again) from Alaska across Asia and Europe and back to the United States, conducting surveys for the nascent system of SAC air bases that would ring the globe. Among his other activities, Lindbergh chaired a committee on air force research facilities, spent two weeks on a nuclear-powered submarine, tested new jets, and flew on B-52 patrols, some of which ventured to the fringes of Soviet airspace. Another of Lindbergh's tasks was to consider ways to increase SAC efficiency. He was well suited for the mission, but his efforts enmeshed him in "the extremely sensitive issues of interservice rivalry."

The nuclear arms race troubled Lindbergh and found him doubting whether an incomparably destructive new war ultimately could be avoided. As a staunch anti-Communist who expressed contempt for both Russia and China, Lindbergh saw no alternative to a buildup of U.S.

strategic forces. The nation needed a capacity sufficient to withstand any attack and retain the capability of massive retaliation. Like most members of the Cold War establishment, Lindbergh focused on the Soviet military threat when the essence of East–West struggle was ideological conflict. Lindbergh shared misperceptions that fueled the militarization of American foreign policy, including the nuclear weapons race that he deplored.

Leaders of the American Cold War establishment found little to criticize about Lindbergh. By 1954 his rehabilitation was complete. In that year, President Eisenhower restored his commission, partly in appreciation of Lindbergh's lobbying efforts in behalf of strategic appropriations, and promoted him to brigadier general in the Air Force Reserves.

When not engaged in consultations for the Air Force, Lindbergh enjoyed spending time with his family. At age forty Anne bore the couple's sixth child and second daughter, Reeve, announcing, to Charles's disappointment, that it would be her last. Anne resumed her writing career, producing another best-seller, *Gift from the Sea*, in 1955. She did not share Charles's strident anti-communism, still kept up with a smattering of left-wing friends, and lacked enthusiasm for her husband's work as a SAC adviser. Although they sometimes spent weeks apart, Charles and Anne remained devoted to one another.

Despite that devotion, their marriage was not free of tension. Their relationship was a traditional one in which Charles was the dominant figure. Anne struggled to balance the demands of homemaking, meeting the needs of Charles and their children, with her own writing career and social obligations. She alluded to some of the frustrations in *Gift from the Sea*, in which she wrote that "Married couples are apt to find themselves in middle age, high and dry in an outmoded shell, in a fortress which has outlived its function." She added that to find her "true center" and "become whole," a woman must "learn how to stand alone." She struck an optimistic tone about relationships near the end of the book in an allusion that may have reflected the adjustment she and her husband made in their own marriage. In a mature relationship, Anne wrote, "The partners do not need to hold on tightly, because they move confidently in the same pattern, intricate but gay and swift and free, like a country dance of Mozart's."

Lindbergh's frequent travels allowed Anne the solitude she needed to pursue her own interests and needs. Once again joining his longtime friend Juan Trippe, Lindbergh resumed his role as a consultant, and later a director, for Pan American Airlines. The aviation pioneer traveled throughout the world, devised means to help promote faster, more efficient international air traffic, and urged Pan Am to convert to jets for commercial aviation. As he had done since the 1920s, Lindbergh remained at the forefront of virtually every major advance in both civil and military aviation.

Despite his untiring efforts to promote advances in aviation, Lindbergh had nurtured doubts since the late thirties about the benefits of technology. Certainly the destruction of World War II and the potential of an even more devastating conflict in the Cold War reinforced those concerns. On receiving the Wright Brothers Memorial Trophy at the Washington Aero Club for "significant public service of enduring value to aviation and the United States" in 1949, Lindbergh called into question the value of technology. He warned that such "progress" carried "the potential to destroy the human race," adding that the material comforts of the modern industrialized world had insulated large numbers of people from the natural environment, which they therefore no longer bothered to protect. The aviator called on humanity to rediscover the "other qualities of life, qualities of body and spirit as well as those of the mind."

In 1948 the aviator published an essay, *Of Flight and Life,* marking his transition from "early confidence in the limitless future of scientific man to an apprehension of the crisis to which a scientific materialism has led him." He warned that "If we do not control our science by a higher moral force, it will destroy us with its materialistic values, its rocket aircraft, and its atom bombs—as it has already destroyed large parts of Europe." Prewar Germany had been a highly developed and cultured society but Germans "turned their backs on the deeper values of their heritage." The lesson was that "If civilization is to continue, modern man must direct the material power of his science by the spiritual truth of his God."

As his hairline receded and Lindbergh advanced through middle age, he became more philosophical and spiritual. He condemned American life as excessively materialistic. "We must stop measuring our standard of life by automobiles, production curves, and dollars of income" at the expense of "simplicity, humility, contemplation, prayer." The aviator, once a religious skeptic, now believed that "While God cannot be seen as tangibly as I had demanded as a child, His presence can be sensed in every sight and act and incident." While still not a formal churchgoer, Lindbergh had discovered his spiritual side.

Of Flight and Life made little public impact and Lindbergh remained almost a forgotten man until his next literary effort reminded a new generation of the reason he had become famous in the first place. In 1953 the aviator wrote *The Spirit of St. Louis,* an autobiographical account of his New York-to-Paris flight that he had been working on for years. Published by Charles Scribner's Sons, the book was an immediate and extraordinary success, garnering its author the coveted Pulitzer Prize in 1954. Lindbergh had invested his narrative with a novelist's pace and style. Despite a lack of formal training, he had taught himself to write better than many professionals by means of his extensive reading, writing, and rewriting. The book was so fluid that some critics hinted that Anne might be the real author, but that was not the case, although she did edit and critique drafts of his work.

Even before the book became a best-seller, the *Saturday Evening Post* paid $100,000 to publish the account in serial form. Lindbergh sold the film rights to Warner Brothers studio for $1 million, but only when it was agreed that his old barnstorming sidekick Bud Gurney would serve as a consultant to supervise the accuracy of the film. Bearing the same title as the book, the film was a major Hollywood production featuring one of the top studio directors, Billy Wilder, and a popular leading man, Jimmy Stewart. Although Stewart was older than the youthful Lindbergh of 1927, he was an admirer of the aviator as well as a fellow pilot and member of the Air Force Reserve. Over the years, the actor and the aviation hero, both tall, lanky, and similar in appearance, became good friends.

The film, offering a romanticized representation of Lindbergh's flight, failed to generate the high attendance Warner Brothers executives had anticipated. Some theater owners expressed reluctance to show it, remembering Lindbergh's Des Moines speech, but no formal boycott emerged. Stewart attributed the disappointing audience response to bad timing and Lindbergh's refusal to assist in promotional efforts. Stewart considered *The Sprit of St. Louis* a good film and believed that he had gotten "right into Slim's character." Lindbergh, however, "didn't help it any. He refused all requests for personal appearances and wouldn't talk to the press."

Lindbergh said little about political affairs in the postwar period. He soured on the Republican party in the early fifties over the excesses of the anti-Communist hysteria associated with Senator Joseph McCarthy, which entailed persecution of thousands of Americans because of alleged Communist sympathies. In 1952 Lindbergh voted for Democrat Adlai Stevenson over Eisenhower. In the 1960s Lindbergh dined at the White House as the guest of President John F. Kennedy, whose enthusiastic support for the National Aeronautic and Space Administration Lindbergh shared.

As Kennedy's successor, Lyndon Johnson enmeshed the country ever more deeply in a futile counterinsurgency war against Communist guerrillas in Southeast Asia. Lindbergh toured Vietnam in 1967 in his capacity as an Air Force brigadier general. Attempting to boost morale, he told reporters that he supported the campaign to fight communism in Asia. Privately, however, he expressed doubts and revulsion at the degrading influence of American culture in Saigon. With Coca-Cola, Marlboro cigarettes, and brothels catering to the American servicemen, it sometimes seemed that little remained of Asian culture in the South Vietnamese capital.

By the late sixties Lindbergh joined many Establishment figures in doubting the wisdom of the American crusade in Vietnam. Although the war took place on "a bad battlefield, badly chosen," he did not think, however, that "we can just step out." He criticized campus rebels and leftists who called for an immediate U.S. withdrawal.

Popular dissatisfaction with the American war in Vietnam contributed to the timing of Lindbergh's decision to publish his voluminous wartime diaries in 1970. Despite his contempt for the news media, Lindbergh was more concerned about his public image than he liked to admit. With protest against the Vietnam War mounting, Lindbergh thought his own opposition to American intervention in World War II might reach a more sympathetic audience. Controversy over his wartime activities had resurfaced in 1966 when Harold Nicolson published his *Diaries and Letters, 1930–1939,* including his observation in May 1938 that Lindbergh counseled appeasement of Germany in part because he "believes in the Nazi theology." Lindbergh responded by demanding an apology and threatening Nicolson's son, Nigel, with a libel suit.

Lindbergh hoped that publication of the 1,000-page book, *The Wartime Journals of Charles A. Lindbergh,* chronicling his private observations from 1938 to 1945, would clarify his views at the time. Lindbergh cut some of the entries for length but he and publisher William Jovanovich noted that no rewriting or extensive editing had been done. Lindbergh realized that some of the entries would prove embarrassing when viewed in light of the passage of a quarter-century, explaining "I could have gone back and cleaned them up but I didn't." In fact, Lindbergh did remove a few of his statements stereotyping Jews.

The book attracted widespread attention and received mixed reviews. Some condemned Lindbergh for what they perceived as his stubborn refusal to admit that U.S. intervention in World War II had been a just cause. In the introduction to the journals, Lindbergh declared that his views had changed little over the years. Even though the United States had "won the war in a military sense . . . in a broader sense it seems to me we lost it." Lindbergh explained that even though Germany and Japan had been defeated, the war had vaulted Russia and China into a position in which they "now confront us in a nuclear-weapon era." Lindbergh refused to admit that he had underestimated the ability of the West to defeat the Axis powers or that he had been insufficiently critical of Nazi atrocities.

Even sympathetic reviewers declined to embrace all of Lindbergh's arguments, but many did commend the journals for the intelligence and strength of convictions that they revealed. Others lamented Lindbergh's preoccupation with race and what some perceived as a reluctance to criticize the Nazis. Taken as a whole, the *Wartime Journals* reveal the inner workings of a complex personality who would not be understood on the basis of the labeling he was so often subjected to throughout his life.

By the early seventies, much to Anne's delight, Lindbergh moderated his position as an uncompromising cold warrior. He still favored a powerful U.S. military force capable of responding to outside threats, but he now agreed that détente (relaxation of tensions) with Russia and China, including nuclear arms control accords, was the most promising path to a safer world.

The shift in perspective, partly a response to changes in world politics, also reflected the anti-technological aspect of Lindbergh's thought, first expressed in *Of Flight and Life*. He stunned many longtime colleagues in aviation by coming out against U.S landing rights for the Anglo-French Concorde supersonic aircraft. For the first time Lindbergh opposed rather than championed a technological advance in aviation, explaining that supersonic jets were unnecessary, uneconomical, a source of pollution, and too noisy.

Lindbergh's doubts about the scientific-technological advance reinforced a lifelong devotion to nature that he had first nurtured during his boyhood in rural Minnesota. By the mid-sixties environmental and wildlife issues mattered more to Lindbergh than aviation or the struggle against communism. In a 1964 *Reader's Digest* article titled "Is Civilization Progress?" he declared that if forced to choose, he preferred birds to airplanes. For years Lindbergh, sometimes with Anne, sometimes alone, had gone to Africa on safari, but he had long since traded in his hunting rifle for a camera, and then carried nothing at all. He and Anne contributed to myriad ecological and wildlife preservation groups, including the Geneva-based World Wildlife Fund, whose executive committee Lindbergh joined. The retired aviator went in search of whales off the Baja peninsula and lobbied for international accords to protect various species.

By the late sixties Lindbergh could be counted on to champion virtually any environmental or wildlife cause. His 1968 speech before the Alaska legislature—his first public speech since the campaign against U.S. intervention in World War II—proved decisive in its revocation of a bounty on wolves. He flew to Indonesia and the Philippines to personally—and successfully—lobby presidents Sukharno and Marcos, respectively, to protect the threatened Javanese rhinoceros and the tamarau, a wild Filipino buffalo. Lindbergh even consented to meet with reporters and photographers if the effort would enhance environmental or wildlife protection. He abhorred television, however, and refused to appear if cameras were present.

Now for the first time in his life, Lindbergh became publicly active in behalf of a popular national cause. He echoed themes stressed by authors such as Rachel Carson (*Silent Spring,* 1962) and Paul Ehrlich (*The Population Bomb,* 1968), who advocated restraint on human development in defense of the natural environment. The environmental protection movement in the United States came of age in 1970, with a national inaugural Earth Day celebration and the creation of the new federal Environmental Protection Agency. Lindbergh endorsed the green movement's advocacy of restraints on development, wilderness preservation, controls on pesticides and other chemical pollutants, and clean air and water legislation.

Lindbergh traveled thousands of miles, lived in primitive conditions, and lobbied in behalf of human as well as animal species. In 1961 he astounded a leader of the Kenyan Masai tribe, who months before had suggested that the aviator ought to see the Masai Reserve, by actually appearing one day amid a cloud of dust from his rented Volkswagen. When Lindbergh announced that he would like to live with the tribe for a time, he received his own private hut and eagerly took to the "traditional diet of fresh milk mixed with blood drawn from the vein of a living cow and served in a gourd rinsed in animal urine." Lindbergh loved to eat whatever local custom dictated no matter where he was, and never complained about the taste or quality of food.

The mounting interest in indigenous cultures prompted Lindbergh's support for PANAMIN—the Private Association for National Minorities—in the Philippines. PANAMIN, directed by a wealthy Harvard-educated Filipino, Manuel Elizalde, Jr., sought to preserve indigenous cultures from development. His efforts in behalf of this group, beginning in 1969, found Lindbergh traveling deep into the Filipino jungles to interact with the people there. In 1971 he went to live among the Tasaday, a group whose way of life had evolved little since the Stone Age. Fascinated by his two-week stay with the lost tribe, Lindbergh compared the exhilarating experience to his 1927 flight. He and Elizalde successfully lobbied President Marcos to set aside land to preserve the Tasaday. Lindbergh lamented that the "insatiable commercial demands" and "fantastic destructive powers" of modern humanity threatened to destroy such a people, as well as myriad animal species across the globe. Again raising the question, "Is civilization progress?" Lindbergh answered that "Living among the primitive always makes me wonder." He realized, however, that the absence of a balanced diet, lack of medicines, and various rituals and taboos rendered these cultures less ideal than they might appear in the romanticized first glance.

Seemingly tireless, Lindbergh stood ready to depart at a moment's notice for an international adventure or lobbying effort. He would merely pack a change of clothes, a toothbrush, and his now regular companion, the Bible, and set off. The famed aviator no longer flew himself, but traveled instead on commercial aircraft, flying tourist class under an assumed name. He expressed contempt for the "sterile" environment of Western-style tourist hotels abroad, declaring that "I would rather sleep in a flophouse with a flea." He often did just that.

When not traveling to exotic locations, the peripatetic Lindbergh spent time with Anne at one of three residences they maintained: a home in Connecticut, a chalet on Lake Geneva, and his personal favorite, a cottage on the Hawaiian island of Maui. The Lindberghs lived simply and relished the natural settings around them. Lindbergh deplored ostentatious living, as reflected in his choice of automobiles—always Fords that he meticulously maintained, year after year, until they no longer functioned.

Despite extensive travels, Lindbergh enjoyed spending time with his children. He had always taken time to play with them during their youth, although he had blended affection with discipline, including corporal punishment. The kidnapping and murder of their first child, which Charles and Anne referred to innocuously as "that business in New Jersey," was discussed so rarely that some of their children first heard about it from their classmates rather than their parents.

All of the Lindbergh children matured and enjoyed success in varied careers. The oldest son, Jon, took his father's advice to eschew a life in aviation, since he could never hope to get out from under the Lone Eagle's shadow. Jon attended Stanford, became a navy frogman, and launched a successful undersea exploration company in Seattle. Land Lindbergh, sharing his father's love of open spaces, moved to Montana, where he managed a cattle company. The third son, Scott, married a Belgian woman and spent most of his time in Europe. Sharing his father's interest in natural species, Scott and his wife raised primates and lobbied in behalf of animal rights causes. The eldest daughter, Anne, became, like her mother, a writer, until she died from cancer in 1993. The youngest Lindbergh child, Reeve, also became a writer and lived in northern Vermont.

Although he turned 70 on February 4, 1972, Lindbergh had more than enough energy to keep up with his children, travels, and activities, often boasting that he never got tired. He even planned a return visit to the Tasaday, for whom he felt lingering affection, but after an Asian tour in 1973 he developed a heat rash and a painful case of shingles. Lindbergh lost a substantial amount of weight, but recovered slowly. On days when he felt up to the task, the aviation hero polished the autobiography he had been drafting for years and which he intended to publish posthumously. *An Autobiography of Values,* gracefully written and philosophical in tone, duly appeared in 1976, two years after his death.

After returning to relative good health and planning to resume his travels, Lindbergh learned after a routine physical examination that he was a victim of lymphatic cancer. Initially there was hope for recovery but some months later his doctors informed him that the cancer had metastasized. Despite their vigorous protests, Lindbergh declined further treatment, bluntly informing his physicians that he refused to die connected to life support systems in a hospital bed.

Never fearful of death, Lindbergh characteristically made meticulous plans for the event, as he had done for all of his great adventures. After writing and calling to say goodbye to family and friends, he flew with Anne and son Land to their secluded residence in Maui. As the recipient of a Congressional Medal of Honor, Lindbergh could have received burial in Arlington National Cemetery, but he chose to be interred in a remote corner of Maui instead. With its lush foliage, gentle breezes, and azure skies, Maui struck Lindbergh as the one unspoiled place in the world. He ordered a simple coffin made of eucalyptus, selected the plain clothing in which he wished to be buried, and even chose the grave site in a small churchyard.

Lindbergh enjoyed the beautiful Hawaiian sunshine and the sound of the Pacific waves rippling onto the Maui shore. Anne Morrow Lindbergh later recalled that her husband's "last ten days were . . . very peaceful and quite timeless." Untreated, the cancer gained momentum. Charles Lindbergh, seventy-two years old, lapsed into a coma and died on August 26, 1974.

Anne became something of a recluse, although she did appear at occasional functions commemorating her husband and his legacy. Sensitive to criticisms of Lindbergh, Anne strove to put in context her husband's wartime activism in interviews and documentary films. She also selected his authorized biographer. After editing and publishing five volumes of her own diaries and letters in the early seventies, Anne did little writing late in life. Troubles continued to plague her, including the death of her eldest daughter and the indictment of her bookkeeper in 1994 on charges of embezzling $136,000 from the Lindbergh estate. By that time Anne had already been incapacitated by a series of strokes. She died on February 7, 2001.

The Lindberghs, once America's glamorous first couple, had long since given way to a new generation and a new style of heroism and celebrity.

Conclusion

Charles A. Lindbergh's life revolved around his status as a hero, a role he never accepted. The controversies that plagued him after his historic 1927 flight derived from his refusal—or perhaps inability—to accommodate himself to the role American society assigned him. Ultimately, Lindbergh destroyed his own exalted public image. To him, it was far more important that he say and do as he saw fit than to mold himself to meet public expectations. Eventually, Lindbergh came to relish bad publicity, which enhanced his own sense that he operated on a higher moral and intellectual plane than the rest of society.

Lindbergh became a hero because he was a courageous visionary in the field of aviation. Captivated by the power and prospect of machines and technology, he visualized the future of air power, with fleets of commercial aircraft linking divergent countries and continents. Lindbergh did more than anyone else in twentieth-century America to make the vision of safe and reliable national and intercontinental air travel a reality.

The heroic solo flight came at a time when the emergence of radio, film, advertising, and consumerism gave rise to the modern celebrity system. People wanted—perhaps, during the Depression years, *needed*—Lindbergh to flash his boyish grin and wave, walking hand-in-hand with his attractive celebrity wife. Although Lindbergh willfully exploited his hero's image to benefit the cause of aviation, he shunned the obligations of fame. He thought he had done his part in the aftermath of the 1927 flight by meeting with politicians and waving to the massive crowds in ticker-tape parades. Thereafter, the onetime solitary Minnesota farmboy, the only child of his parents, wanted to get "out of the hero business" and be left alone to pursue his adventures, business interests, and family life. But the public could not get enough of him. Denied his right to privacy, he grew surly and resentful.

Lindbergh could not accommodate what the public expected of its heroes, especially following the great tragedy of his and his wife's life, the 1932 kidnapping and murder of their infant son, Charles, Jr. The crime was, of course, a direct result of Lindbergh's celebrity. The wrenching series of events—the horrifying discovery of the empty crib, the notes and ransom payment, the discovery of the baby's body, the subsequent investigation, and the trial of Bruno Richard Hauptmann—all were accompanied by a never-ending series of flashbulbs popping in Lindbergh's face, rumors, lies, and half-truths printed and stated over the airwaves. By the time photographers broke into the morgue to snap shots of his dead son, and began to terrorize his second child in an effort to snap pictures of him, Lindbergh had had enough. He took his family to live overseas.

The New York-to-Paris flight, in so many ways a heroic triumph, was in just as many ways a curse. It not only produced unwanted celebrity, but also encouraged Lindbergh's own hubris. By doing what no one had done before, by accomplishing alone what the experts said should not even be attempted, Lindbergh began to view his own judgment as infallible. His confidence was such that he even contemplated unlocking the secrets of life and death in his experiments with Alexis Carrel. Subsequently, he became convinced that his controversial views on national and world affairs were the correct ones. He did not seem to understand, however, that public affairs could not be counted on to operate with the surety of a carburetor.

When Lindbergh felt passionately about a subject, whether it was aviation or U.S. foreign policy, he stated his views bluntly. Late in life, he told a Briton whom he had offended during the war years, that "Everybody used to call me Silent Slim, but I guess there were times when I said a damn sight too much for my own good." He was self-educated and tended to see issues in simple, though nonetheless often perceptive, terms.

Lindbergh was an intensely private public man. The whole concept of public relations disgusted him. He made no effort to give the key interview or publicize his decisive efforts to promote Robert Goddard's experiments, or his World War II exploits. Early on Lindbergh concluded that "It would be necessary to sell my character if I wished to maintain the friendship of modern journalism." He "preferred its enmity." He was, as he admitted, "just a stubborn Swede" who was as willing to challenge the Establishment as his father and grandfather had been before him.

The vicious debate over U.S. intervention in World War II ultimately destroyed Lindbergh's heroic image in the United States. When the war broke out in Europe in the fall of 1939 the aviator had already become an expatriate. Scarred by tragedy, he blamed not just the press but American society. The nation, mired in the Depression, was too frivolous, too permissive, too prone to manipulation by politicians such as Roosevelt, as Lindbergh saw it, to be a leading force in world affairs.

The expatriate Lindberghs led a solitary existence on their estate in Great Britain, but traveled and read widely. Lindbergh evolved his judgments about the European countries at the very time that war threatened to engulf the continent. Britain and France he dismissed as declining powers. He considered Russia backward and governed by a fanatical regime. In contrast, Lindbergh viewed Germany as an orderly society where a man could maintain his right to privacy. On his visits to Germany, carefully orchestrated by the Nazis, he saw a nation with a strong sense of national purpose and the destiny to occupy a leading position in Europe. A Social Darwinist, Lindbergh believed that the rise of Germany represented the survival of the fittest, the outcome of an inevitable historical process.

Successful in calling attention to the rise of German air power, Lindbergh nonetheless exaggerated the power of the Luftwaffe. Worse, he badly misjudged the essential character of a Nazi regime that would leave the world in smoldering ruins. Lindbergh was not the only Westerner, by any means, to misjudge Hitler's Germany, but he did seem prepared to believe the best about it and the worst about the Western democracies. By 1938, when terrorism against Jews and other groups became state policy in Germany, Lindbergh began to perceive the essence of Nazism. By that time, especially since he already had received the medal from Hermann Goering in the U.S. embassy, the aviator's reputation as a German apologist had been firmly established.

Although after 1938 he became increasingly sober in his perception of Nazi Germany, Lindbergh insisted that the West should avoid at all costs a war whose only result would be the destruction of Western civilization. Despite the intense vilification heaped on him at the time—and by historians and biographers since—Lindbergh's position had a logical foundation. He called for Britain, France, and the United States to remain neutral while Germany and the Soviet Union weakened each other in a battle for Eastern Europe. Such an approach would have given the democracies the time they needed for rearmament—of which Lindbergh was an outspoken advocate—so that they might be prepared in the event of a westward Nazi advance. By promising war with Hitler over Nazi aggression in Eastern Europe, he argued, Britain and France encouraged Berlin and Moscow to collaborate, a process that culminated in the 1939 Nazi–Soviet Pact, followed by Hitler's offensive against Western Europe.

Once the European war erupted, Lindbergh advocated a negotiated settlement. He remained haunted by the parallel he drew with the ancient Peloponnesian wars that destroyed Greek society. He predicted the same fate for Europe. Lindbergh therefore threw himself passionately into the anti-interventionist movement, displaying as much courage in public affairs as he had in the air.

The aviation hero had argued persistently, based on his firsthand observations, that German military power surpassed that of its European rivals. He was correct, as Hitler's *blitzkrieg* triumph across continental Europe demonstrated. Ultimately, both key events of 1941— Hitler's foolish decision to open a two-front war by invading the Soviet Union in June and American intervention in December—were required to defeat Nazi power. The aviator accurately predicted that millions would die in the war. On the other hand, Lindbergh badly underestimated both Britain's capacity to withstand the German air offensive and the ability of the democracies, including his own country, to mount a punishing war effort of their own.

Contrary to the charges of his critics, however, neither naiveté about Germany nor moral cowardice explained Lindbergh's opposition to U.S. intervention. Rather, he believed the greatest contribution the United States could make to maintaining "civilized life" would be to remain out of the horribly destructive war and serve as a model of peace and prosperity. Lindbergh thus embraced classical ideals of American foreign policy, which held that the United States should avoid intervention and "entangling alliances." In *Of Flight and Life,* Lindbergh echoed George Washington, Thomas Jefferson, John Quincy Adams, and others, by declaring that American foreign policy would succeed "less by forcing our system of democracy on others than by setting an example others wish to follow; less by using arms than by avoiding them; less by pointing to the 'mote' in another's eye than by removal of the 'beam' in our own." To Lindbergh, the improvement of American life was "more important than the spreading of it. If we make it satisfactory enough, it will spread automatically."

Lindbergh and his America First colleagues argued that U.S. intervention would not result in a democratic Europe. After the war, they cited Soviet domination of half of Europe as evidence in support of their argument. They also predicted that Washington would be required to devote enormous resources to maintaining peace on the continent. The Truman Doctrine, the Marshall Plan, the North Atlantic Treaty Organization, and other programs did entail vast U.S. investments to provide for European recovery and security.

Above all, Lindbergh and the advocates of America First warned that intervention would erode democratic idealism both at home and abroad. In foreign affairs, much as they feared, the United States, acting as a world power in the postwar years, supported a variety of dictatorial and oppressive regimes. The emergence of a national security state and an "imperial presidency" found the United States intervening in peripheral conflicts around the world, including Korea and Vietnam, spending record amounts on defense, punishing opponents of these policies at home, and fueling a nuclear arms race.

These were precisely the undesirable consequences that Lindbergh warned would result from the abandonment of traditional neutrality in favor of U.S. intervention in the

European war. In the period leading up to Pearl Harbor, Lindbergh and his anti-interventionist colleagues sought open debate, accurately charging that Roosevelt was exaggerating threats and misleading the public to build support for U.S. intervention. Unwilling to settle for a democratic debate of the issues, the Roosevelt administration went to great lengths to discredit its opponents. The administration savaged Lindbergh, even questioning his loyalty, because, as a popular hero, he represented the greatest threat to the interventionist agenda.

Unfortunately, Lindbergh had left himself vulnerable to attack. He frequently criticized the Western democracies, yet was reluctant to condemn the fascist powers. Even worse, Lindbergh's stereotypical comments about Jews in his Des Moines speech diverted attention from the merits of his anti-interventionist argument, at a crucial point in the national debate, and left him vulnerable to charges of anti-Semitism. Lindbergh's stubborn refusal to moderate his language, even at the urging of his wife and close associates, shows the extent to which he had become alienated from the culture that had once venerated him.

Lindbergh was too complicated a man simply to be dismissed as a fascist, racist, or anti-Semite. He did, however, harbor stereotypical beliefs about Jews and nonwhite peoples. Lindbergh did not hate Jews, nor favor discrimination against them, but he exaggerated their influence and separateness from mainstream America. As his support for indigenous cultures in the postwar period suggested, Lindbergh was hardly a visceral racist and later spoke out in advocacy of civil rights for African-Americans.

As a young man coming to maturity in the age of the automobile and the airplane, Lindbergh evolved an innocent but profound faith in progress. During the pioneering age of aviation, he "felt sure airplanes would bring peoples of the world together in peace and understanding."

To see the airplane instead emerge as a source of unprecedented destruction in World War II was a cruel blow that left him disillusioned. "Why, I ask myself, should I spend my life developing aviation if aircraft are to ruin the nations which produce them? Why work for the idol of science when it demands the sacrifice of cities full of children; when it makes robots out of men and blinds their eyes to God?"

Ultimately, Lindbergh was a tragic figure whose transformation reflected the grim realities of the violence of twentieth-century life. Instead of ushering in a new age of progress and brotherhood, scientific advances created unprecedented destruction, excessive materialism, ecocide, and a severing of connections with the natural world.

While World War II destroyed Lindbergh's faith in progress, the conflict also brought him relief. Opposition to U.S. intervention had tarnished Lindbergh's image and made him a fallen hero. Although he could never hope to lead a normal existence, Lindbergh found fewer flashbulbs exploding in his face, less harassment of his family, and more freedom of movement than he had known in the prewar period. He was finally free to play the role of a free-thinking eccentric who had more in common with like-minded individuals such as Alexis Carrel and Henry Ford than with the man in the street.

Lindbergh will be best understood as an uncompromising American individualist. He was truly a lone eagle, a man who pursued his own interests and stated his views with little regard for how those actions might be perceived by the public at large. He was stubborn, and sometimes wrong, but he displayed a fierce integrity and unquestionable courage.

When Lindbergh's individualism found him refuting conventional wisdom and accomplishing the solo New York-to-Paris flight, the public celebrated him. When that same individualism found him expressing his controversial opinions about world affairs, the press and public condemned him. That was the irony of Lindbergh's life. The nation exalts the individual whose timely deeds fulfill a psychic need, but just as eagerly sets out to destroy those who stand in the way of its mass compulsions. In its romantic myths, the United States celebrates the rugged individualist; in reality, it does so only selectively.

Study and Discussion Questions

Chapter 1: The Lindberghs of Minnesota

1. What was life like for immigrants coming to the United States? What does the injury suffered by Lindbergh's grandfather suggest about life on the frontier?

2. What positions did C. A. Lindbergh take up after entering into Minnesota and national politics? How successful or unsuccessful was he?

3. Discuss young Charles's attraction to machines and technology. What was it like to travel around the United States by automobile in the pre-World War I era?

Chapter 2: Wings of Destiny

1. Discuss the appeal of aviation during its formative years. Why were young men (and later women) like Lindbergh so attracted to aviation that they were willing to risk their lives?

2. What hazards did Lindbergh face in carrying the U.S. mail by air?

3. What do Lindbergh's determination, planning, and execution of the New York-to-Paris flight tell us about his personality? What type of person was he?

Chapter 3: The Hero

1. How do you account for the tumultuous reception of Lindbergh after his epic solo flight to Paris? Why were people, especially in the United States, seemingly so desperate to celebrate heroism?

2. In what ways did Lindbergh seek to exploit his fame to the benefit of commercial aviation? How did he benefit personally, economically, and commercially from his fame?

3. What did Lindbergh dislike or resent about becoming a public figure? Was it unrealistic of him to expect to be able to lead a more private life in the wake of his heroic flight?

Chapter 4: Crime of the Century

1. What did Charles and Anne Morrow see in one another? To what extent do you think Lindbergh's attitudes about marriage differ from those of today?

2. What can be learned about the capabilities of local, state, and federal law enforcement from the Lindbergh baby kidnapping and the subsequent investigation? How did the kidnapping spur change in federal law?

3. Considering the Hauptmann trial, how would you evaluate the justice system of the era? Did Hauptmann receive a fair trial? How much influence do you think Hauptmann's German ancestry and the public desire for vengeance had on the outcome of the trial?

Chapter 5: Expatriate

1. What kind of person was Anne Morrow Lindbergh? How unusual do you think it was for her to cultivate such skills as a pilot and to accompany her husband on myriad international aviation adventures? Are you surprised the couple left their children for such long stints of time?

2. What attracted Lindbergh to men like Alexis Carrel and Robert Goddard? In what ways did he help these men with their research?

3. How did Lindbergh come into conflict with President Franklin D. Roosevelt?

4. To what extent can you sympathize with Lindbergh's decision to take his family and leave the country? Do you think he could have handled the situation any other way?

5. Why did Lindbergh spend so much time in Germany? What about German culture attracted him?

Chapter 6: America First!

1. Why did Lindbergh oppose U.S. intervention in World War II? What did he think the consequences would be?

2. Analyze the way in which the Roosevelt administration responded to Lindbergh and its implications for democratic debate on foreign policy.

3. Was Charles Lindbergh an anti-Semite? How do you explain his comment about Jewish people in the United States?

4. What were the goals of the America First Committee? Were its positions and concerns legitimate? Did Lindbergh help or hurt the cause?

Chapter 7: After the Fall

1. How did Lindbergh maneuver to involve himself in the U.S. war effort despite his previous opposition to intervention?

2. How did Lindbergh's attitudes about aviation and technology change in the postwar era? What explains this change of perspective?

3. How do you account for Lindbergh's growing concerns about the global environment? Why do you think he was so attracted to indigenous cultures?

4. What do you think of the way Lindbergh chose to handle his illness and impending death?

Chapter 8: Conclusion

1. How would you assess the author's overall conclusions about Lindbergh and his life? Do you agree with his conclusions?

2. What do you make of the author's final point about the United States celebrating individualism only when it conforms with mainstream views and punishing it when it does not?

A Note on the Sources

By far the most complete account of Lindbergh's life is the comprehensive authorized biography, *Lindbergh* (New York: Berkley Books, 1998), by A. Scott Berg. The author received privileged access to the Lindbergh Papers at Yale University's Sterling Library and received the cooperation of the Lindbergh family. Another recent biography, *Anne Morrow Lindbergh: Her Life* (New York: Nan A. Talese, 1999), adds to our knowledge of the Lindberghs as well.

The Lindberghs' own writings remain an invaluable source to understanding their lives and times. The books *We: The Famous Flier's Own Story of His Life and Transatlantic Flight* (New York: G. P. Putnam's Sons, 1927) and *The Spirit of St. Louis* (New York: Charles Scribner's Sons, 1953) inform not only about the historic 1927 flight but also about the aviator's background and character as well. The slender volume, *Boyhood On the Upper Mississippi: A Reminiscent Letter* (St. Paul: Minnesota Historical Society, 1972), written late in his life, is a nostalgic look at his early years in rural Minnesota. The best single source written by the man himself is his comprehensive and posthumously published *An Autobiography of Values* (New York: Harcourt Brace Jovanovich, 1976; rev. eds., 1977, 1978). Often overlooked, the essay *Of Flight and Life* (New York: Charles Scribner's Sons, 1948) bridges Lindbergh's years as an aviation pioneer, and champion of science and technology, to the more philosophic musings of his postwar years. *The Culture of Organs* (New York: P. B. Hoeber, 1938), co-authored with Alexis Carrel, discusses Lindbergh's medical research at the Rockefeller Institute.

Anne Morrow Lindbergh's voluminous writings illuminate travels, family life, and her public philosophies. Her diaries and letters constitute five volumes. *North to the Orient* (New York:

Harcourt Brace, 1935) and *Listen! The Wind* (New York: Harcourt Brace, 1938) are the best sources on the Lindberghs' aerial survey adventures in the 1930s. Anne's controversial *The Wave of the Future: A Confession of Faith* (New York: Harcourt Brace, 1940) is important for understanding the Lindberghs' perspectives on fascism and war on the eve of U.S. intervention in World War II. *Gift from the Sea* (New York: Pantheon Books, 1955) addresses, if only obliquely, her relationship with Charles, as well as the challenges to women in American society. Reeve Lindbergh's roman à clef, *The Names of the Mountains* (New York: Simon & Schuster, 1992) is suggestive on Lindbergh's character and on the Lindbergh marital relationship. Dorothy Herrmann, *Anne Morrow Lindbergh: A Gift for Life* (New York: Ticknor and Fields, 1992) is a fine comprehensive biography.

Other than Berg's authorized account, biographies of Lindbergh fail to capture the essence of his character. Among them are Joyce Milton's *Loss of Eden: A Biography of Charles and Anne Morrow Lindbergh* (New York: Random House, 1993); Leonard Mosley's *Lindbergh: A Biography* (New York: Doubleday, 1976); Walter S. Ross, *The Last Hero: Charles A. Lindbergh* (New York: Harper & Row, 1976); and Brendan Gill, *Lindbergh Alone* (New York: Harcourt Brace Jovanovich, 1977). All Lindbergh biographers have benefited from the foundation laid by Kenneth S. Davis in *The Hero: Charles A. Lindbergh and the American Dream* (New York: Doubleday, 1959). Another useful source is Tom D. Crouch, ed., *Charles A. Lindbergh: An American Life* (Washington, DC: National Air and Space Museum, 1977). Perry D. Luckett's *Charles A. Lindbergh: A Bio-Bibliography* (New York: Greenwood Press, 1986) is an essential guide to the literature.

Other sources illuminate Lindbergh's forebears and early life in Minnesota. Bruce L. Larson, *Lindbergh of Minnesota: A Political Biography* (New York: Harcourt Brace Jovanovich, 1973) is the definitive work on the career of Lindbergh's father. Carl H. Chrislock, *The Progressive Era in Minnesota, 1899–1918* (St. Paul: Minnesota Historical Society, 1971) places the senior Lindbergh's activism in scholarly context.

An abundant literature places Lindbergh in the context of the history of American and world aviation. Joseph J. Corn, *The Winged Gospel: America's Romance with Aviation, 1900–1950* (New York: Oxford University Press, 1983), brilliantly locates attitudes about aviation in the American cultural tradition. Also useful is Roger E. Bilstein, *Flight in America, 1900–1983: From the Wrights to the Astronauts* (Baltimore: The Johns Hopkins University Press, 1984). Richard P. Hallion, Jr., *Legacy of Flight: The Guggenheim Contribution to American Aviation* (Seattle: University of Washington Press, 1977), discusses Lindbergh's business ties and promotion of commercial aviation.

Lindbergh's own *The Spirit of St. Louis* (New York: Charles Scribner's Sons, 1953), winner of the 1954 Pulitzer Prize, can never be displaced as the best account of the historic New York-to-Paris flight. Unsurpassed in explaining the dramatic impact of Lindbergh's flight on the American public is the classic article by John William Ward, "The Meaning of Lindbergh's Flight," *American Quarterly* 10 (Spring 1958): 3–16.

Also useful is Dixon Wecter, *The Hero in America* (New York: Charles Scribner's Sons, 1941).

The saddest chapter of the Lindbergh story, the kidnap and murder of his infant child, has been told in depth in *The Lindbergh Case* (New Brunswick, N.J.: Rutgers University Press, 1987; reprint, 1994) and in a comparative analysis in my own *Murder, Culture, and Injustice: Four Sensational Cases in American History* (Akron, OH: University of Akron Press, 2000). George Waller, *Kidnap: The Story of the Lindbergh Case* (New York: Dial Press, 1961) is outdated. Serious students of the history will want to read the actual transcripts of the trial, which comprise a compelling case for Hauptmann's guilt, in Sidney B. Whipple, *The Trial of Bruno Richard Hauptmann* (New York: Doubleday, 1937). Less serious students can consult the ever-growing volume of fatuous conspiracy-theory literature.

On Lindbergh's surveys of German aviation in the 1930s, an essential source is Robert Hessen, ed., *Berlin Alert: The Memoirs and Reports of Truman Smith* (Stanford, CA: Hoover Institution Press, 1984). On the Luftwaffe's deficiencies, see Ronald Lewin, *Hitler's Mistakes* (London: St. Edmundbury's Press, 1984).

By far the best analysis of Lindbergh's views about Nazi Germany and his opposition to U.S. intervention in World War II is Wayne S. Cole, *Charles A. Lindbergh and the Battle Against American Intervention in World War II* (New York: Harcourt Brace Jovanovich, 1974). Cole's *Roosevelt and the Isolationists, 1932–1945* (Lincoln: University of Nebraska Press, 1983) is also indispensable. For Roosevelt's perspective on the issues, see Robert Dallek's sympathetic *Franklin D. Roosevelt and American Foreign Policy, 1932–1945* (New York: Oxford University Press, 1979). Justus D. Doenecke, *In Danger Undaunted: The Anti-Interventionist Movement of 1940–1941 As Revealed in the Papers of the America First Committee,* is a splendidly edited documentary history.

Geoffrey S. Smith, *To Save a Nation: American Countersubversives, the New Deal, and the Coming of World War II* (New York: Basic Books, 1973), and Leo P. Ribuffo, *The Old Christian Right: The Protestant Far Right from the Great Depression to the Cold War* (Philadelphia: Temple University Press, 1983), provide context on the political and diplomatic controversies of the Depression era. Harold Nicolson, *Diaries and Letters, 1930–1939* (New York: Atheneum, 1966), is a personal, and sometimes damning, account by Lindbergh's one-time British friend. The aviation hero's own 1,000-page personal account, *The Wartime Journals of Charles A. Lindbergh* (New York: Harcourt Brace Jovanovich, 1970), is a highly revealing source on Lindbergh's character and antiwar activism.

More study needs to be done on Lindbergh's postwar career, including his service with the Strategic Air Command, views on the Cold War, environmental activism, and defense of wildlife and indigenous human cultures.

Index